A FRIEDMAN GROUP BOOK

Published by GALLERY BOOKS
An imprint of W.H. Smith Publishers, Inc.
112 Madison Avenue
New York, NY 10016

ISBN 0-8317-0424-1

THE ART OF ARRANGING ARTIFICIAL FLOWERS
Creative Decorating with Gorgeous Floral Look-alikes
was prepared and produced by
Michael Friedman Publishing Group, Inc.
15 West 26th Street
New York, New York 10010

Designers: Rod Gonzalez and Barbara Goodman
Production: Karen L. Greenberg

Gallery Books are available for bulk purchase for sales promotions
and premium use. For details write or telephone the Manager of
Special Sales, W.H. Smith Publishers, Inc., 112 Madison Avenue
New York, New York 10016. (212) 532-6600

Typeset by BPE Graphics, Inc.
Color separations by Hong Kong Scanner Craft Company
Printed and bound in Hong Kong by Leefung-Asco Printers Ltd.

WITH GREAT APPRECIATION, THE AUTHOR ACKNOWLEDGES:

Ada Lambert
Carol Popkins
John Deane
Karla Olson
Laurant Garnier
Rose
Sophie Bouton
Anthony Viteritti
Ned Zink

CONTENTS

INTRODUCTION
PAGE 6

INTRODUCTION

The spectacular artificial flowers of today, recreating nature magnificently with their luxuriant and lifelike appearance, are transforming and revolutionizing floral design. A new, animated world has been discovered, where hundreds of species of the most stunning flowers and foliage and fabulously lush evergreens, trees, and potted plants, mirror and, in many instances, surpass their natural counterparts. With nature as the model, each artificial flower, leaf, and plant, has been carefully studied and designed, and materials and colors have been impeccably chosen so that as much truthfulness as possible has been achieved.

Finely crafted, high-quality artificial flowers recently have nurtured a phenomenon in interior design as well, as people discover that entire rooms and homes can be designed around their brilliance, beauty, and permanence. Here, the exterior landscape has been brought inside, creating a new,

natural—and faultless—interior environment.

Real flowers, because of their fragility, expense, and short life span, were previously only an "added attraction" to the design features of any room or home, unable to sustain a permanent role. But with the nearly imperceptible falsity of today's artificial blooms, the glamour and excitement of nature can be coordinated with wallpaper design, fabric texture and colors, and furniture styles to attain a breathtaking effect that is, in all respects, permanent.

Rooms where flowers only occasionally accompanied the decor now feature year-round, magnificent bouquets of luscious roses, spectacular varieties of lilies, small baskets overflowing with tiny daffodils and miniature irises, and fabulous trees, with limbs and leaves hanging in the perfect position for display. Totally coordinated in color, design, style, and texture for a special, surprisingly vibrant effect, the artificial flower has now become the focal point in these sensational rooms, bringing them to life by creating a continually exhilarating ambience.

The durability of this remarkable "new nature" makes designing easier and more appealing not only for professional floral and interior designers but for the home designer—the do-it-yourself person—as well. With real floral arranging, a mistake—a stem cut too short or petals accidentally pulled off during arranging—is usually either costly to correct or uncorrectable. But the strength and adaptability of artificial flowers invites you to use them courageously to decorate your own home environment.

Artificial flowers, buds, stems, leaves, and foliage can be repaired in seconds, saving the expense of replacement and the frustration of failure. With artificial floral design, you can build your own magnificent creation, step-by-step, changing any part of the design effortlessly, without being fearful of damaging the flower. Or you can rearrange the same flowers for a totally new and refreshing look.

Imagine the satisfaction you will feel when your own stunning creation, bursting with color and life, is displayed in your home. You will witness it lifting the spirits of all who enter.

The lush photographs and informative text contained in this book invite you to explore this *nouveau monde*. With the clear, step-by-step design information and instruction here, every room in your home can be made exciting and vibrant.

You will notice that an immense, colorful bouquet of garden flowers will bring the "outdoors in" and evoke nature's freedom and joy. An elegant, formal arrangement will highlight any traditional or Continental period decor and create a showcase for antiques and works of art, just as a free-flowing, massive, contemporary arrangement will open the room to the celebration of life. Whatever the style, the decor, or the period, whatever the ambience or the mood, the information here will show you how the artificial flower can and will fulfill your desire for a new *art de vivre*.

THE BASICS OF ARTIFICIAL FLOWER ARRANGING

THE ELEMENTS AND PRINCIPLES OF FLORAL DESIGN

Floral design is highly personal, an art that reflects each arranger's creativity and special floral tastes. Yet, whether you use artificial flowers or fresh ones, the success of an arrangement is achieved by attention to the elements and principles of floral design. These design guidelines, which are defined in detail in this chapter, are generally agreed upon by floral designers throughout the world and are evident in every arrangement—artificial or real. At this time, your eye is probably accustomed to seeing only the overall effect of a good design. However, by learning and applying the elements and principles of good design correctly, you'll begin to recognize how each element and principle is deliberately applied. In any arrangement, some are weighted more heavily than others, depending on the flowers employed and the results desired. Experiment by creating several arrangements that focus on a specific element or principle or a combination of them. Soon you will understand the effects possible from the emphasis of one element or principle and how they all work together.

THE ELEMENTS OF DESIGN

Five basic elements of design are at work in any successful arrangement. They are form, space, line, texture, and color.

Form is the geometric shape of an arrangement. Every arrangement is created from one of several basic forms: the triangle, the circle, the line, the curve, or the angle; each of these will be discussed more extensively later in the chapter. The elements within the form are height, depth, and width.

Space is the void between each flower. This space accentuates the individual beauty and importance of each bloom, leaf, and branch—highlighting each part within the total effect of the arrangement. As in a constellation of stars, space creates a pattern where all parts are individually spotlighted, yet work together toward a harmonious concept.

Line is the skeletal framework within the form of the arrangement. The type of line employed gives the arrangement the definition of shape

An explosion of vertical lines creates a fireworks effect in this stunning contemporary arrangement. The deep purple and lavender irises, and the purple and pink scabiosa are dramatically accented by an ingenious use of space. The long, vertical stems are left exposed and, therefore, become an integral part of the arrangement's design. Cleverly, the magenta field thistle and the elongated pink gayfeather are used to lighten the arrangement, while harmoniously emphasizing the vertical movement. Finally, the vertical lines nestle in a bed of white baby's breath and pink alpine forget-me-nots.

A wicker basket brimming over with summer flowers welcomes summer into the home. This low, dense, oval arrangement achieves its planned effect through the blend of light floral colors that fill all the available space in and around the container. The design is balanced and compact, with no lone blooms escaping from the container or the arrangement. A wicker basket is chosen as the container, in keeping with the natural theme. The soft pinks of the yellow-centered anemones and the spotted alstroemeria are softly contrasted with the white colchicum, forget-me-nots, and other alstroemeria. Maidenhair greenery provides a natural buffer between the flowers and the container and continues the brimming effect. A country dinner table or a summer patio would be especially brightened by this arrangement.

that is necessary regardless of style. Circular, oval, and crescent designs employ curved lines, while horizontal, vertical, and angular shapes use straight lines. In many contemporary designs, the line element may be made more important than the form, or it may be used to emphasize the principles of accent or color. For example, a triangular arrangement featuring roses and lilies may have eucalyptus branches radiating from the basic form in lines that reach beyond the limits of the shape. The overall effect of the line element is to highlight the tighter form of the arrangement and the roses and lilies.

Texture is the surface quality of the flowers, leaves, branches, container, and accessories in any arrangement. The high quality of artificial flowers means their textures are rich and lifelike, so texture can be featured as prominently as with fresh flowers. Most arrangers create harmony (a principle to be discussed later) by blending similar textures. Silky roses, for example, are best displayed in porcelain, not in a cane basket. However, many Oriental and contemporary designs deliberately use contrasting textures to add drama to the arrangements.

Color, used and selected correctly, is the final essential element to every successful floral design. Color is forceful and potent, the most evocative component of design. It will rouse or cool emotions in the viewer, creating a mood and a reaction. The sweetness of spring, the vibrancy of summer, the dazzle of autumn, the sparkle of winter, all live permanently with artificial flowers that provide color and beauty year-round, warming hearts during the chilly winter and encouraging the thaw in spring. (See Chapter Three, "Color Is Key," for more about the importance of color.)

THE PRINCIPLES OF DESIGN

The principles of design are the arranger's reflection on the tenets of nature. Arrangements, like their naturally growing sources, should embody balance, unity, accent, harmony, rhythm, and scale. Each of these prin-

In this contemporary arrangement, form and contrast are dramatized for special effect. The round form of the arrangement is mirrored in the crystal container, and the large white magnolia in the center are effectively contrasted by the surrounding forget-me-nots. A cluster of yellow sweet William and white-and-yellow alstroemeria lightens the outer edges, bringing depth to the entire arrangement.

ciples is an integral part of every arrangement, from a formal mass to a contemporary line design.

Balance is what gives the arrangement its sense of being weighted correctly. Large, dense, or dark-colored flowers positioned toward the middle of the design establish the center of the arrangement. Lighter-colored or smaller flowers, buds, and foliage should then radiate outward from this center. An arrangement like this will have balance and will look as if it can stand on its own. In formal designs, symmetrical balance is achieved by flanking the center line of the arrangement with exactly equal blooms, foliage, and accessories. Asymmetrical balance looks properly weighted without the use of repetition. For example, the darkest-colored flowers are placed low and to one side in the arrangement, near the top of the container to create a solid base. These flowers are balanced by a group of lighter-colored flowers that thrust out to the opposite side of the base, and several wispy branches that reach high up, straight from the base.

Unity is the sense of wholeness attained when the arrangement's individual components—flowers, foliage, container, and accessories—work together, creating the effect that they belong together. The permanence of artificial flowers allows you to create an ever-changing yet highly unified artwork, where blooms can be shifted or altered easily for variety or seasonal adaptation without disturbing the accord of the arrangement.

Accent is usually the dramatic focal point, calling attention to and stressing certain areas of interest within an arrangement. Accent is created with a flower of a dominant color, size, or shape, placed in what becomes the visual center of the arrangement. The lighter blooms, buds, and foliage will move outward or upward from this center. A single large dahlia, for instance, is an accent when placed at the focal point of an arrangement of smaller flowers because it is preeminent. Sprinkle a few lavender alstroemeria throughout a sea of pink alstroemeria, and the lavender becomes the accent of the pink.

Accent is often created in an arrangement by contrasting materials with each other for an enhancing effect. Repeated use of the same ingredient will leave your arrangement looking tired and dreary, lacking the life that is natural to all flowers. Just a touch of contrast in color, texture, foliage, flower shape, or leaf shape will provide the accent necessary to catch the viewer's eye.

Harmony is the successful contrast and blend of the components in the arrangement. An arrangement, for example, of pink and white magnolias with line or spike flowers, such as purple delphiniums or gladiolus, filled out with Queen Anne's lace is a harmonious blend of shapes and colors.

Rhythm is the flow of flowers, foliage, and color in an arrangement, blended for a smooth transition from each component to the next. Rhythm suggests movement, usually from larger to smaller flowers, from darker to lighter colors. The rhythm of an arrangement takes the viewer's eye away from the focal point, all around the design, then back to the focal point, where the visual cycle starts again. In many contemporary ar-

Perfect for warming a bare corner, this mass arrangement of similarly colored flowers will dominate its setting. Tall burgundy and purple larkspur spikes reach upward, establishing the correct proportion. A wave of light blue irises changes the color tone and shifts the movement downward to the right. This rhythm is echoed by the bright yellow buttercups, which move from left top to right bottom, and the purple bougainvillea in the right-hand corner. All this movement is created by the focal flowers—the giant pink peonies—that are massed in the bottom left corner like a rock over which the other flowers cascade.

Stunning visual harmony between flowers and surroundings has been achieved in this Oriental montage. A giant red lotus, effectively accented by its own giant leaves, dominates the setting. A few white orchids and wild thistle aspire heavenward to complete the earth-man-heaven symbolism of ikebana design. The container is perfect in its neutrality, and the oval mirror, Oriental chest, and ashtray are harmonious accessories.

rangements, there may be no specific focal point but rather a series of related points, rhythmically flowing and working together to carry the eye through the arrangement.

Scale is the creation of the proper proportion of all parts of the arrangement. Basically, the principles of scale are common sense. Small or miniature flowers are best displayed in a small vase. Tiny, delicate lilies of the valley would be lost in a large vase. Majestic gladiolus would be unattractive and overpowering in an undersized vase. Scale is also the harmonious blend of flower sizes. Dahlias, magnolias, and hollyhock assemble together amicably, but giant hydrangeas would dominate small, delicate almond blossoms.

All of these elements and principles are employed in varying degrees in every floral arrangement. Whether your design is country, Victorian, Oriental, or contemporary, the elements and principles play the same roles, providing the same effects. Whenever you create an arrangement, take a moment to look at it with each of these components in mind; make

sure they are all working together properly, and every design is guaranteed to be a success.

DESIGN FORMS

As discussed earlier, any flower arrangement is based on forms derived from several three-dimensional geometric shapes—triangles, circles, lines, angles, and curves. Some of these shapes, especially lines and curves, will at times be used with other shapes for very dramatic designs.

Line Designs

Simple, vertical lines aspire upward. They can be symmetrical, as in a tall, straight, contemporary arrangement flanking a doorway, or they can be asymmetrical, as in a graceful ikebana design set alone in an alcove. Horizontal lines are low and spread long. Their base or accent must be firm because of the low center of gravity; therefore, horizontal line designs are stable and peaceful. They are particularly effective when they grace a

This carefully balanced arrangement gives the casual impression of a freshly picked bunch of country flowers. The lovely red tulips sparkle from the arrangement's center, their color contrasting with the blue forget-me-nots and the spiked plumes of white forest hyacinth that surround them. Wild orange and raspberry foliage and branches are scattered throughout the arrangement to add balance and to continue the country motif. The carafe vase was chosen to further the impression that the arrangement was "just picked."

dining room table, for they provide all the impact of a lovely centerpiece without impeding conversation. They also work extremely well on mantels and sideboards, and just below a hanging mirror or painting.

Angle Designs

Angle designs are derived from lines. The right or left angle is a combination of a vertical and a horizontal line. One side may be longer than the other. There is no line between their two outer points, and the space between the lines is left empty. Angles work well as accents on the sides of a painting, statue, or mirror. The inverted "T" is an angle variation that uses a minimal number of flowers and foliage very effectively.

Triangular Designs

Symmetrical triangular designs are formed by placing two right angles back to back and filling the space inside. Easily balanced with any flowers, the symmetrical triangle is formal and elegant. It is seen most often in traditional settings, sometimes on a pedestal for added dignity.

Asymmetrical triangular designs are closer to nature, for they are unevenly balanced on both sides as flowers might grow outside. Therefore, they are very popular in contemporary design, which often attempts to imitate natural settings.

Combining two triangles, one ascending, the other descending, will form a diamond pattern that is popular for wedding bouquets, banquet arrangements, and funeral displays. Many of these are stunning when displayed from a pedestal.

Circle Designs

Circle designs can be large or small, but they are usually full and are meant to be viewed from all sides. Many centerpieces are circular. If special care is taken to place flowers so they radiate from the center of the arrangement, magnificent depth can be achieved in this form. The round form can be adapted to traditional and contemporary tastes by simply adjusting the circumference flowers to create a smooth or rough silhouette. Certain flowers can be highlighted by positioning them so they

violate the circle design.

Oval or Oblong Designs

Oval and oblong designs should be placed in longer areas, such as on the dining room table, on a long sideboard, in a window area, or on a mantel. The shape will visually fill the space, and is tremendously effective if the scale of the arrangement is carefully proportioned to the area. Oval and oblong designs should be at least one-quarter and not more than one-third the length of the display area.

Cone Designs

The rounded triangle of the cone-shaped design is meant to be viewed from all sides and, therefore, has depth and density. This arrangement is perfect for a small area, such as on an end table. The Christmas-tree-like shape flows gently and evenly upward, tall but not too wide.

Crescent and Curve Designs

Crescent and curve designs are similar to right angles, except that they

Harmony and accent are the key in this gentle round arrangement featuring white carnations. The rich depth and texture of each bloom is brought forth by the contrast with the muted, pink tones of the clusters of sweet William that surround them, and the matching pink ceramic vase. The wispy baby's breath and twinkling white forget-me-nots softly outline the shape of this composition. The floral picture is a harmonious blend of flowers that soothes and relaxes the viewer.

The triangular form is cleverly displayed here in a stark ikebana design. A low, flat black dish contains three yellow irises positioned at different heights metaphysically representing heaven, man, and earth. Green iris leaves brighten the yellow iris blooms and carefully accent their fragility and exquisite beauty. A few bare fruit branches reach "heavenward," emphasizing the basic triangular shape of the arrangement. An erratic vine placed in the lower half of the arrangement adds a touch of mystery. The whole arrangement flows from flower to flower with a wonderful rhythm, each of the minimal number of components integral to the overall effect.

are curved and tilted at an angle. The flexibility of artificial flowers makes them perfect for this simple, graceful, flowing shape. This style is very adaptable to Oriental, as well as traditional themes; simply choose appropriate types of flowers, and place them carefully within the design. The crescent is best displayed in a low dish on a pedestal for a sense of greater drama.

The Hogarth curve is an "S"-shaped design that is a natural for artificial flowers. Though exceptional beauty can be created in the "lazy S" line with a minimum of materials, many real flowers lack the flexibility required to be bent into position. However, with artificial flowers, you can create an unlimited number of glorious Hogarth-curve designs. It is usually arranged in a tall container that accentuates the sweep rhythm of this form. The Hogarth curve is sometimes seen running between two intertwined circles, in a display that represents romance and friendship.

For added drama and effect, circles and lines can be mixed together. A circle arrangement of roses and car-

nations, for example, might be placed on top of a horizontal line of lilacs. A contemporary design might feature hydrangea, hanging over a container's edge in curved lines, while the upper portion of the arrangement displays orchids and anemones with cattails spiking outward at all angles in a roughly circular design.

The key to successful arranging is to pay special attention to the elements and principles of design, but also to be bold and daring in creating your arrangements. Simplicity is usually striking in its effect, but never be afraid to develop these forms. Today, the elements and principles of floral design are being redefined by the tremendous versatility and adaptability of artificial flowers and foliage. They can be set in more patterns and shapes than natural flowers. Flowers that were rarely arranged together, because they were of different seasons, are being spectacularly and refreshingly combined. Breathtaking floral arrangements are enhancing rooms all year. You are on the threshold of new and innovative design. Let yourself be creative and adventurous.

This fiery mass of scarlet, crimson, pink, and burgundy sets an otherwise uninteresting, neutral corner ablaze with hot floral color. A contemporary circular arrangement featuring giant crimson cosmos with deep yellow centers mirrors the colors found within a flame. Curves of pink freesia and scarlet wild centaury flare in opposite directions, spreading the visual heat from window to dresser top. Deep within the arrangement, burgundy ranunculus and black and red berries intensify the crimson cosmos. These dramatic colors are cooled with green and maroon foliage. These leaves create a wall between the flowers and the deep red ceramic container. Without this shield the container would be too intense and would dominate the arrangement. The "heat" of this design spreads to the adjacent lamp. Patches of multicolored forget-me-nots appear to be smoldering on the lamp itself. The lampshade also comes alive. Notice how the shapes and colors rythmically flow and stand out against the neutral background of window, wall, and furniture.

DETERMINING SIZE AND STYLE

Creating an arrangement of the correct size and style is a critical factor in its success. All your creative energy will be wasted if your design is too big or too small for its setting; if the style clashes with the interior design of the room where it appears; or if the flowers and vase you choose are

This contemporary arrangement demonstrates the importance of space in floral design. With stark simplicity, a few white marigolds are arranged at different heights, imparting individual importance to each bloom.

not appropriate for the design, style, and size of the finished arrangement. Your lovely design will be ruined by any of these fatal flaws.

To ensure that none of these design disasters ever occur, think carefully before you begin to arrange, or even to choose the elements for your display. To determine the correct size and style of any floral arrangement keep these three factors in mind: (1) the size of the space where you have chosen to display the arrangement; (2) the interior design of the display area; and (3) the types of flowers and containers you have available for your arrangement.

These three factors are obviously related, for the style of the decor will help to determine the type of container and flowers that are compatible, and the size of the area will dictate the size of the arrangement and therefore the size of the container you will use to fill the space. In any event, before you begin putting together any arrangement, take a few moments to carefully consider these factors. You will much more successfully achieve the proper balance between them in the design relationship you create.

SIZE

The size of the area you have chosen for the display will determine the general size of your arrangement. For example, a low alcove with a tiny table in it should feature a small, oval arrangement of roses and anemones. A group of lofty snapdragons would overwhelm such a compact area, but would look breathtaking in the corner of a foyer with cathedral ceilings.

Once you have determined the general size of the arrangement, choose one of the design shapes discussed in Chapter One to fill the space. In large, open spaces, mass designs in circular and triangular shapes are effective. The empty corner of a room is perfect for a wonderful Victorian display featuring a huge amount of flowers in a giant vase set upon a pedestal. The artificial, and therefore permanent, arrangement would be like a lovely sculpture in its crowning effect. A large, formal, triangular arrangement would fit perfectly on the end of a couch, set against the wall. It would fill the space that usually displays a painting with refreshing creativity. In a small space, such as on a mantel or

This massive Victorian bouquet of monochromatic color tones is well-suited to any large setting, such as a bare corner with an empty wall behind it. The size of the arrangement also demands that it be set on a pedestal or a fairly large table. The tall, spiked larkspur establish the design proportions in all directions: upward, outward, and downward. Giant pink peonies lend their mass and visual weight to the arrangement. The delicacy of the pink freesia and tiny wild asters contrast with the giant peonies. Foliage is inserted in the unfilled spaces for color contrast and to complete the full, mass effect of the design. In an arrangement of this magnitude, the designer must have a heavy, secured container that will not topple over. Some floral designers will fill the container halfway with sand to make sure the arrangement is stable.

As if just delivered from the florist, these stunning Paris roses in a clear glass container epitomize the modern style. The bouquet of roses is arranged cleanly with no embellishment. The stems are clearly seen through the container, an integral part of the simple style; the flowers almost appear to be standing on their own. On a table or buffet against a white wall, these roses require no accessories to bring a brilliant flash of color to the room. Best of all, this bouquet of beautiful red roses will never wither or fade.

Once you have determined the general size of the arrangement, choose one of the design shapes discussed in Chapter One to fill the space. In large, open spaces, mass designs in circular and triangular shapes are effective. The empty corner of a room is perfect for a wonderful Victorian display featuring a huge amount of flowers in a giant vase set upon a pedestal. The artificial, and therefore permanent, arrangement would be like a lovely sculpture in its crowning effect. A large, formal, triangular arrangement would fit perfectly on the end of a couch, set against the wall. It would fill the space that usually displays a painting with refreshing creativity. In a small space, such as on a mantel or a tiny table, employ a simple horizontal or curved design to showcase the flowers without taking much room in height and width. A few vibrant hibiscus blossoms floating in a bowl will be stunning, yet will fit the space limitations.

A tall, narrow space calls for a vertical line design or the aspiring motion of a Hogarth curve. Both of these designs flow upward, giving the impression that they cover more space than they do. Many of today's contemporary homes have high ceilings and high walls that must be filled with imaginative arrangements. A very unusual but beautiful effect will be created by a reaching vertical arrangement of extra-long quince branches, pussy willows, and cattails arranged in a striking narrow urn. Place the arrangement near a window, and sunlight will cause the branches to cast long shadows up the wall and onto the ceiling. For evening, place a small spotlight at the base of the arrangement facing up into it. The dramatic thrust of this line design will be extended by the shadows so that even the tallest wall is filled with eye catching shapes and lines.

STYLE

Determining the style of your arrangement is a delicious exercise that will help you to choose the flowers and container you will use. The style of the room dictates the type and color of the flowers in the arrangement and their container, as well as determining the decorative theme of your design. Continental, Victorian, Colonial, Oriental, and contemporary are the most common decorative styles. Each one suggests traditional flowers, shapes, and other elements. However, artificial flowers are available in so many new colors and species that you will find yourself creatively extending the design specifications of these themes. A Victorian display of lilacs, for example, used to be limited to a few colors—lilac, pink, and white. With artificial flowers, that Victorian display will burst with green, blue, and deep purple as well.

Below are basic descriptions of each of the most common design styles. But let yourself go when you put together your display. Explore the new expression that the greater availability of artificial flowers allows you.

An artificial floral designer used only a few materials very cleverly in this congenial display. The climbing green-and-white triangle of cyclamen and its foliage was created by splitting a large cyclamen branch into its individual components, and giving each one a separate stem. The leaves and flowers are then bent into the shape that will joyfully fill a small window or wall area. As a result of its simple, airy appearance, this arrangement will blend neutrally with any style of interior design.

25

Here, again, we see the marvelous technique employed by artificial floral designers, who realize that they can split a solitary blossom to create new and revolutionary blooms. A giant rhododendron flower has been broken up, each piece given an individual stem, and then all of them arranged starkly in a shallow, footed bowl. Orientally influenced, this design has been carefully crafted to create a "wild rhododendron" rising from a bed of leaves. While simple and small in scale, this composition is dramatic and will make an impact on any setting.

You're likely to be astonished at the combinations you'll come up with.

Continental is a French style established between 1600 and 1800. Floral arrangements from this period were usually formal, symmetrical circles and triangles. The flowers traditionally used were lilacs, tulips, sweet peas, daisies, carnations, and roses—all in pale shades of blue, pink, yellow, cream, white, and green. Favored containers were classical, alabaster vases; glass, silver, and bronze bowls; and porcelain urns. Though actual antique containers are breathtaking to use today, many inexpensive recreations are available at artificial-flower markets and floral supply stores.

The Victorians placed flower arrangements everywhere, whether there was room for them or not. Massive, dark displays of hydrangea, larkspur, lilacs, dahlias, roses, hyacinth, and cornflowers were packed in elaborately detailed vases and other containers of porcelain and bronze. Small arrangements crammed with grape hyacinths, daisies, nasturtiums, and anemones were scattered on every available open surface. Little attention was paid to "arranging" during this period; the emphasis was on the display of a variety of flowers.

The degree of formality in a Colonial American floral arrangement was often dependent upon the arranger's social and economic status. Daisies, geraniums, sweet william, and all varieties of wildflowers were displayed in pewter and copper jugs, kettles, cups, ladles, and wooden bowls in simple, country homes. The more elegant homes featured large, formal, triangular designs with irises, daisies, snapdragons, roses, pansies, and sweet william in large porcelain tureens. Pewter, copper, and brass containers were also used. In either place, there was a distinct lack of floral options; the Colonists had little time to cultivate flowers and made do with what was growing naturally in their area. However, the containers were as varied as any of the vessels found in a Colonial home. Today, you can use any flowers for these arrangements if you use an indicative container.

Simplicity and symbolism are the most prominent features of Oriental style in interior design. Ikebana is the highly structured art of floral arrangement that is reflective of this decor. It mirrors the natural world through artful designs of flowers and foliage positioned to represent

This impressive Victorian arrangement brings a continental flavor to an eclectic setting. The massive height and depth of the larkspur are especially appreciated when arranged with many giant, white anthurium. Yellow daffodils and red centaury impart color and feeling to what would otherwise be a very plain arrangement. When viewed from a distance, the shape of the larkspur petals reflects the strokes of the impressionist painting on the wall.

A lovely, formal, triangular arrangement of irises, crocuses, and baby's breath is perfect for an elegant dining room table. The soft colors—purple, pink, and white—are blended in an airy, gentle design that will not overwhelm your dinner table or your guests. Each blossom has been carefully spaced for individual emphasis and so it will not block anyone's view. Only a few baby's breath are used as filler flowers. Again, a technique only possible with artificial flowers has been employed in the arrangement; solitary crocus blooms have been taped onto a single stem, creating a branch that does not exist in nature.

heaven, earth, and man. Only a few flowers are used in symbolic placement, accompanied by stark branches and foliage. Usually, this is done by using material in groups of three. Three imperial roses and three quince branches appear at the different levels of the heaven-man-earth trilogy. Driftwood, stones, interesting rocks, unusual shells, and other accessories are then incorporated into the design for a natural effect. Fruit branches, Fuji mums, irises, and lilies are some of the most common ikebana floral elements, but you can substitute any flowers into the triadic framework without loss of meaning.

Contemporary is the most difficult style to characterize. Contemporary features are constantly changing, as today's tastes change frequently. Generally, contemporary style features the eclectic mix of other design schemes and the manipulation of all their rules to find new expressions. For instance, a contemporary arrangement may feature a Continental design in a traditional round shape. However, space in the contemporary design will be used to emphasize the individual importance of each compo-

This is a traditional circular arrangement, perfect for a coffee or dining table. The yellow chrysanthemums are the focal flowers. They are the brightest of the soft colors and are positioned in the most prominent place. They are complemented by the gentle pinks of the orchids, lilies, and alstroemerias scattered throughout, but always within the circular form. Finally, a few white rosebuds and happy forget-me-nots fill in the spaces in this lovely design.

nent instead of focusing on the mass, as is usual in a Continental design. This is where the versatility of artificial flowers is usually liberating. The blooms and stems can be bent and twisted into any position without damage, so new shapes and forms can be adopted.

Contemporary style is also characterized by the skillful blending of vastly different textures, shapes, and colors, often freely arranged to reflect the way the elements are found in nature. The contrasts create a visual rhythm that keeps the eye moving from bright colors to soft pastels, from smooth-textured blooms to harsh, spiky branches, exploring the arrangement for rules and familiar features. To fascinate the viewer with a unique design is the ultimate goal of the contemporary style.

Many established rules are being bent today. It used to be that a dinner-table arrangement never could be designed so high that the diner's view across the table was impeded and conversation was awkward. Traditionally, these arrangements are not over twelve inches in height. A contemporary table arrangement, however, may

This arrangement is a perfect example of the importance of balance. The designer has displayed a spreading bouquet in a surprisingly small pot. The trick, however, is to position the blooms out, not up, so the container-to-display ratio is correct. Also, the darker-colored flowers are bunched in the middle with lighter blooms on the outside, making the arrangement appear solidly anchored in the middle. Careful attention to the principle of balance is the success of this design.

rise as high as twenty-eight inches (seventy centimeters), but will be open and airy enough to permit viewing and conversation through it. Imagine your guests' surprise when you display an arrangement of graceful apple branches flowing airily outward and upward over their heads, symbolizing nature's own designs.

Contemporary designs utilize every species of flower and foliage while updating traditional arrangements and breaking new design ground. The vast variety of artificial flowers and their consistent availability makes them the perfect medium for contemporary design. Contemporary style is clean and graceful, yet striking, bold, and dramatic. Creative freedom is the most important element in successful contemporary design.

TYPES OF FLOWERS

After deciding the arrangement's general shape, size, and style, it is time to select the artificial flowers that are best suited to your intended design. Artificial flowers—like real ones—can be categorized by their shapes into three groups: line flowers, focal flowers, and filler flowers.

In this arrangement, poinsettias, often just a Christmas flower, are used in a contemporary spring design. A yellow container, instead of green or red, makes the flowers much brighter. The asymetrical triangle form is a new twist on the traditional symmetrical triangle form as well. Finally, the flowers are complemented only by bushy thistle, a very unorthodox partner for poinsettias. The overall effect, only possible with artificial flowers where poinsettias are a year-round possibility, is breathtaking.

The list below is an abbreviated inventory that will assist the designer in determining the appropriate flowers and their function in an arrangement.

LINE FLOWERS	FOCAL FLOWERS	FILLER FLOWERS
Apple blossom	Amaryllis	Acacia
Cattail	Camellia	Anemone
Cherry blossom	Carnation	Aster
Firethorn	Chrysanthemum	Bleeding heart
Forsythia	Daffodil	Bougainvillea
Gladiolus	Dahlia	Buttercup
Hollyhock	Fuji mum	Cedar
Honeysuckle	Gardenia	Cosmos
Horsemint	Hibiscus	Daisy
Hyacinth	Iris	Forget-me-not
Larkspur	Lilac	Freesia
Lavender	Lily	Heather
Liatris	Magnolia	Heliotrope
Lupine	Marigold	Huckleberry
Manzanita branch	Orchid	Maidenhair
Peach blossom	Peony	Mimosa
Pussy willow	Poinsettia	Mountain laurel
Quince branch	Rose	Queen Anne's lace
Snapdragon	Tulip	Ranunculus
Stock	Zinnia	Silver-lace vine

Line flowers are tall, straight flowers, such as larkspur, gladiolus, and fruit branches. When placed in an arrangement, these flowers form the skeletal framework. Artificial flowers are particularly appropriate for this purpose because they can be twisted and bent easily to fit the backbone of the design shape required. With real flowers, you must search for a bloom or branch that is the right shape and height, then often settle for something close to what your mind's eye envisioned but not quite right. On the other hand, you can bend artificial snapdragons into the exact sweeping "S" that is the basis for your Hogarth-curve arrangement.

A rule of thumb when using line flowers is that the tallest flowers or branches should be placed so that they extend one-and-a-half to two times above the container. A twelve-inch- (thirty-centimeter-) high container will require branches reaching eighteen to twenty-four inches (forty-six to sixty centimeters) above the mouth of the vase. Any taller, and the arrangement will look out of balance and might topple. Any shorter, and the container will be too prominent,

GENERAL RULES OF ARRANGING

Once you have decided on the size, style, and specific flowers you will use in your design, there are some rules that will make assembling your arrangement easier. They are not ironclad but are listed here for basic guidance. Your personal style and taste will dictate how much you adhere to them.

RULE 1. Establish the skeletal shape of an arrangement by first setting the line flowers and/or foliage in place. Next, set the focal flowers within the design, placing each one for individual emphasis. Finally, use the filler flowers to complete the arrangement by filling in unwanted empty spaces.

RULE 2. Dark-colored or heavy blooms should be placed toward the physical and visual center of an arrangement to ensure proper balance. If placed toward the outer framework of the design, they will give too much visual weight to that area. Obviously, focal flowers are usually the heaviest and darkest-colored blossoms.

RULE 3. Wherever possible, use an uneven number of flowers for balance. Generally, one flower provides the primary focal point, then an equal number of the same flower are displayed on either side to provide balance.

RULE 4. Similar flowers should be placed at different levels in an arrangement rather than at one height. This will give individual importance to each bloom.

These suggestions and rules are a guide for the beginning floral designer. As you gain designing experience, you will deviate from these guidelines and use your imagination and your eye instead.

and the arrangement will appear bottom-heavy.

Focal flowers are the single-blossomed flowers used as the visual focal point in an arrangement. Roses, dahlias, peonies, and carnations are examples of these flowers. Focal flowers are usually positioned at the center of the arrangement, and they are often of a striking color and shape. They become the visual center by virtue of their shape, weight, and prominence.

Filler flowers are employed to cover the empty spaces in the arrangement without stealing the limelight from the focal flowers. Queen Anne's lace, forget-me-nots, and ranunculus are small, bushy-headed blooms that fit these design requirements. Filler foliage includes any of the flowers in the chart at left.

COLOR IS KEY

Color, because of its visual diversity, is the ultimate deciding factor in the success or failure of every floral arrangement. It is the key that breathes life into your design and elicits the desired, planned-for, emotional response from the viewer. The thematic effect of color on the mind's eye can be cooling and peaceful, hot and passionate, joyful and exhilarating, or tranquil and serene.

The artificial flowers of today are successful because of their ability to capture nature's striking colors in their fabric dyes. The brilliant shades and tints not only mirror nature to perfection, but they magnify it by allowing rich color design and surprising combinations all year round.

WHAT IS COLOR?

It is essential to have a basic understanding of the creation of colors, tints, shades, and tones, in order to blend them properly in floral arranging.

Red, yellow, and blue are the three primary colors. The secondary colors—orange, violet, and green—are created from various mixtures of the three primary colors. Primary blue mixed with primary yellow will yield secondary green, while red and blue will produce violet, and red and yellow will mix into orange. These six colors are the basis of the color wheel. By blending a primary color with a secondary color an intermediate color is created. For example, mix yellow, a primary color, with green, a secondary color, to create yellow-green, an intermediate color.

Tints are achieved by adding white to a color. For example, red with white added to it will produce pink, a softer and more feminine tint of the original color. Shades are achieved by adding black to a color. Take red again and add black to create maroon, a denser, more masculine color. Tones are the mixture of gray with a color. When gray is added to red, dusty rose is obtained, a color that is a little more neutral and slightly less feminine than pink. The tints, shades, and

The sophisticated elegance of this arrangement is created through the skillful use of color tints and contrasting textures. The delicate peach color of the hibiscus and orchids at the heart of this design would fade into the foliage if the giant white peonies were absent. Instead, the large white areas provide enough contrast to attract attention to the subtle colors of the peach-colored blooms. The creamy sweetpeas, Queen Anne's lace, and white centaury further enhance this subtle contrast. This arrangement is likely to be found on a formal dinner table amidst silver and crystal, where its understated sophistication would be superb.

Here, rich red flowers are made even more intense by the bold touches of yellow that surround them. The yellows atop the tall snapdragons in the center of the primula and ranunculus, and in the large, round yellow ceramic container are brilliantly balanced so that they frame the hot red. The dark-green foliage fills out the design without curtailing the flaming effect of the red and yellow flowers.

tones of a single color can be blended in a floral arrangement for a striking, harmonious effect. For example, in a room with a background color that is a tint, such as a pink room, design a stunning arrangement of maroon, dusty rose, and pink.

THE COLOR WHEEL

The color wheel shows you the primary, secondary, and intermediate colors and their relationship to each other. Notice that the primary colors, the secondary colors, and the intermediate colors are equidistant from each other on the wheel. It is also important to understand the characteristics of the three primary colors and three secondary colors before discussing various color combinations, so that there is a basis for your selection of colors in an arrangement.

Primary Colors

Red is a hot color associated with passion, romance, and vivacity. It is used abundantly at Christmas, on Valentine's Day, and during the summer in bouquets and arrangements featuring crimson red roses, all transmitting expressions of love and caring.

Blue is a cool, subdued, yet stately color that evokes a peaceful mood from its viewers. The effect of a bunch

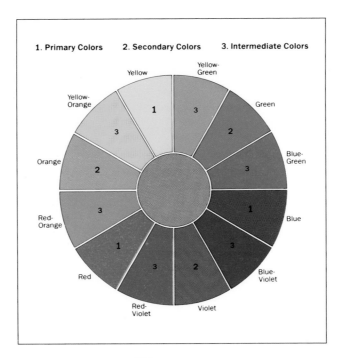

Brilliant red hibiscus are stunning in this arrangement of complementary colors. The result is a warm, heartening combination striking in its natural simplicity. The flowers appear almost as they would in a field, cushioned in a bed of greenery. A few well-placed buds continue the effect, and the lighter, orange freesia, stretching forth at the peak of the arrangement, resembles a newly born blossom reaching for the sun.

of blue larkspur in a blue jug set on a porch is soothing and comfortable.

Yellow, reflecting the elements of the sun, is joyful and lively. Yellow daffodils and golden buttercups fill any room with sunshine.

Secondary Colors

Orange, a blend of red and yellow, is a less vigorous mixture of the emotions of those two primary colors—passion from red and joy from yellow. Brilliant orange marigolds or tawny day lilies add zest to an arrangement but with a touch of the crispness of autumn.

Violet, consisting of blue and red, is a harmonious blend of contrasts. In a bunch of irises, the blue values give peace, coolness, and dignity, while the red offer a depth and regality.

Green is directly opposite hot and passionate red on the color wheel, a combination of blue and yellow that invites a cool, relaxing response. Its prevalence in nature is a reflection of its vitality and liveliness, though it can never be overbearing.

This spectacular mix of analogous colors—red, pink, and purple—with tints and shades creates a rich, contemporary design. The color scheme allows a diverse mixture of floral types: pink peonies, magnolia, larkspur, delphinium, and rhododendron, purple irises, red dahlias, and white lilacs, morning glory, and dahlias. The careful juxtaposition of each flower keeps the eye moving rhythmically and joyfully through the arrangement.

Here is a monochromatic blend of purples that celebrates the subtle tones and shades of this color. Informal in design, the regal, purple-tinged irises and royal pink dahlias are surprisingly well complemented by the wild larkspur, lilac, primula, striped petunia, and sanguisorbas. In a contemporary twist, grass fronds are scattered throughout the arrangement to extend the perimeters and encourage movement in all directions. In this intricate design, the eye is constantly moving from one flower to another, discovering the vastly different shapes and textures that were not apparent at first glance. The viewer's eye first sets on the colors, then after a moment discovers the depth of shape and texture.

CLASSIC COLOR COMBINATIONS

Floral arrangers around the world are familiar with the implied characteristics and sentiments of the different colors. They also have a basic understanding of the four classic color combinations—monochromatic, complementary, triadic, and analogous—and the different emotional message each transmits.

Monochromatic Design

Monochromatic design is the use of a single color and its own tints, shades, and tones. Here, the most intensely colored blooms are usually the focal point, with the lighter shades and tints moving outward in the arrangement. A monochromatic design has a happy, peaceful effect because it embodies harmony within itself and with the surrounding area. For example, an arrangement in various shades, tints, and tones of purple, in a pale lavender vase, would blend gorgeously into a pink bedroom.

Complementary Design

Complementary design is the use of flower colors that are directly opposite one another on the color wheel and on the emotional spectrum. The depth and sincerity of contrasting showy red with cool green is often felt at Christmas, in arrangements of poinsettias and evergreens. Glowing orange marigolds and peaceful blue larkspur suggest the warm stillness of summer, while sunny yellow daffodils and subdued violet irises herald the coming of spring. All these combinations are obviously complementary because the magnificent differences between the two colors and the way the two colors affect one another evoke an emotional response all their own.

When designing a complementary arrangement, make sure one color dominates as the focal color. Support the dominant color with blooms in its shades and tints, then add just a few of the complementary flowers. Choose flowers of similar textures to

This warm, monochromatic arrangement of yellow tulips, irises, chrysanthemums, primula, and buttercups is ready for the kitchen table. The sunshine in these flowers offers greetings and cheer in the morning as the day begins.

allow the contrast in color to be the most evocative element of the arrangement.

Triadic Design

Triadic design employs colors that are equidistant from one another on the color wheel, such as blue, red, and yellow, or orange, green, and violet. These are especially appealing designs today because the use of bold colors is dramatic and contemporary. With neutral filler flowers and a black vase, triadic color designs make a stunning statement, one that immediately awakens the viewer with the startling fireworks effect of the colors and the emotions.

Analogous Design

Analogous design is the use of three or four colors that are next to one another on the color wheel. Red, orange, yellow, and green are warm and thrilling. There is no conflict between their color values because each color is an extension of the others. All four work together to reflect and blend

A mix of flowers and fruit in an ikebana-inspired design is perfect for a contemporary living room colored in warm earth tones. The irises and marigolds have been deliberately spaced to enhance the accent of each flower and to cool the intensity of their bright yellow. A few delicate forsythia and mimosa clusters serve a dual purpose as filler flowers and as the creators of a gentle movement within the design. The lemons and other fruits at the arrangement's base add weight and new textures, an Oriental characteristic.

43

Blue and violet forget-me-nots in a deep blue vase are strikingly accented by the creamy color and unusual textures of lunaria branches. Forget-me-nots are technically a filler flower and are usually not displayed by themselves. However, their primary color is intensified when set against the cream-colored flowers. Alone, the delicate forget-me-nots are not exciting. With the addition of the lunaria, however, a stark contrast is created that gives them depth and charm.

with each other's values. Analogous design is the most popular design employed today because it allows for the use of a variety of colors, but is also visually harmonious.

Remember that when using three or more colors in any design, you should keep a proportion of sixty percent light-colored flowers, thirty percent medium-colored flowers, and ten percent dark-colored flowers. The dark-colored blooms have more visual impact, so this will give an overall balance and movement to the design. Too many dark colors will overshadow the design and make it seem top-heavy and dense.

Choosing the colors for an arrangement becomes delightful when you understand the effects and subtleties of different colors and combinations. However, these rules only provide a basis and a beginning. Experiment with your favorite colors and flowers in different combinations. Be daring, then enjoy the results when a small corner or a whole room comes alive with color and feeling.

The harmony of complementary colors is apparent in this display of chrysanthemums, agapanthus, and thistle. The pastel yellow of the chrysanthemums is sharpened when displayed against the backdrop of the lavender agapanthus. Larger dark purple agapanthus blooms are placed at the center of the arrangement, from which the pale yellow chrysanthemums and the lavender agapanthus move upward. The lavender agapanthus were created by breaking apart a large bloom and taping several components evenly spaced on one stem.

45

CHOOSING A CONTAINER

The astonishing colors, breathtaking hues, and complex textures that are blended to perfection in quality artificial flowers and foliage fulfill their carefully planned purpose when they are properly displayed in the appropriate container. The correct container performs a large variety of tasks within the setting of a design. A container can add a touch of class and elegance, create a mood of romance or drama, contrast with or embellish the flowers it holds, or balance and harmonize flowers and foliage with the environment where the arrangement appears.

Often flowers need little other embellishment when they are placed in a carefully chosen container. A tall, simple, pale yellow glass, filled with a few white daffodils of various lengths needs only one or two pieces of greenery to add a delightful warmth and cheeriness to a cozy breakfast nook. The container plays a vital role in an arrangement such as this, which has very few components and, therefore, takes a minimum amount of effort to design.

Containers that succeed in a variety of arrangements are usually simple, classically shaped, unadorned with designs, and of soft, muted colors. They have the versatility to blend with the various styles of a house and numerous types of floral designs and will enhance—never challenge—the supremacy of the flowers they hold. For example, a softly colored lavender ceramic vase can be employed for an arrangement featuring deep purple irises and pink chrysanthemums. The complementary shade of lavender will create a stunning background and enrich the tones of the irises and chrysanthemums by emphasizing the depth and subtlety of their colors.

On the other hand, a gorgeously designed, Victorian mass of brilliant blossoms would be destroyed if placed in a high-tech, acrylic container. The paradox of flowers with container would violate the harmony and joy of the flowers, as well as be visually displeasing. Always take special care to make sure the container is in sync with the overall design scheme.

In Oriental design, the container is more integral to the arrangement and is often more visible in the design. This low, black dish, a type often used in ikebana-inspired arrangements, substantially but unobtrusively holds the giant peonies. These blooms aspire toward heaven, symbolizing man's quest for immortality. The container is solid and secure and easily supports the large massive blossoms as they move upward.

A popular trend in modern design is to fill a glass container with colored marbles, letting the container provide the dazzling color contrast. The marbles also provide ample support for the flower stems. Here, yellow tulips are coupled with pale turquoise marbles. The result is a "new wave" color combination that surprises as much as it pleases the viewer.

FACTORS TO CONSIDER

When searching for the correct container, you will usually decide first what flowers you are going to use in a particular arrangement, and whether your design will be contemporary or traditional, Continental or Victorian, Oriental or modern. These decisions will narrow the choices of shape and color when you select the proper container. You should also consider texture and its relationship to the arrangement when you choose a vase, bowl, pot, or basket. An enamel cachepot is perfect when filled with glossy foliage. The texture of the pot blends well with the foliage and will showcase the center attraction—the foliage—without overwhelming it. In a different arrangement, you might employ the container as a point of textural contrast, adding interest and diversity.

Setting and decor should also, in part, dictate the type of container used in a particular arrangement. A room with a country theme demands

White daisies placed in a stunning, painted basket need nothing more to come alive. The colors of the basket make it as important a component in the design as any flower would be. Yet, neither the basket nor the daisies dominate the arrangement. Instead, they work together with balance and contrast. The texture and shape of the daisies stand out against the soft pastels in the basket. The whole arrangement has a country feeling of nature providing simple wonders for our pleasure.

a selection of terra-cotta vases, highly textured and unusual baskets of wicker, woven thatch, and grapevine, and some simple, ceramic bowls that will blend with the setting in style and texture. A traditional or Continental period room would be perfectly accompanied by large formal arrangements in fabulous Wedgwood and sparkling crystal vases, Delft bowls and bricks, and ornate compotes and goblets. Less formal traditional and Continental period settings are magnificently accentuated by pewter pots, Limoges cups, antique bottles, and cast-iron cookware.

The modern line design is well displayed in medium-sized containers utilizing popular contemporary colors, such as gray, beige, pale green, off-white, and black. The best containers are usually oval with low bases.

Oriental gentleness and the subtleties of ikebana design require a variety of low containers for differing effects. Shallow dishes and plates, and flat, wooden burls are appropriate for Moribana designs, where accessories are an integral part of the arrangement. You will also need tall, striking vases and glasses, and deep containers with high pedestals for tall, Nagiere-style arrangements.

If you use a patterned vase, make sure that one color in the vase is dominant and that it matches the dominant color in your arrangement. Choose outstanding, larger flowers for the focal point of your arrangement so that the similarities between flowers and vase are highlighted, not contrasted.

Clear containers are stunningly beautiful and effective when used with artificial flowers and accessories. For instance, a large display of calla lilies and green foliage in a clear container is striking and forceful. Some flowers will need to have their stems hidden with solid-colored glass marbles or stone chips, but you can use the elements to enrich your design. These accessories position the flowers effectively, hold and hide the stems, and emit a brilliant, sparkling luster that adds vitality to any contemporary arrangement.

Often the shape of the flowers will help you decide on the shape of the container necessary for proper display and arrangement. Spiky, tall, line flowers, such as snapdragons, gladiolus, and cattails demand a container tall enough to support these statuesque flowers, both physically and visually. Round flowers, such as peonies, magnolias, and Fuji mums require a container that will highlight each blossom as the feature attraction. For example, a low, open bowl is the perfect place to exhibit a few simple magnolia blossoms. The flaring neck of the bowl reflects the open thrust of the flowers, highlighting their delicate shape.

TWELVE BASIC CONTAINERS

There are twelve basic containers that are ideal for all floral styles and designs. Every home designer should have a basic inventory of them for use with any arrangements. The twelve containers are compotes; cylindrical vases; shallow, oval bowls; shallow bowls with an attached base; deep bowls; deep bowls with an attached

A French contemporary mixture of gentle pastels is wonderfully displayed in this lavender container. The height of the arrangement, established by the soft, peach hibiscus bloom, is correctly proportioned at one-and-a-half times the height of the container. The container, darker than the flowers, provides bottom weight. The smooth, ceramic surface is a perfect complement to the variety of textures in the flowers.

51

A lacquered wicker basket holding a large group of apple blossoms is an example of a neutral container that contributes to the desired effect. The apple blossoms have been gathered in appreciation of their simple, colorful beauty. The container enhances them without attracting attention to itself. A few striped petunias hanging over the side of the container reflect the two-tone color of the basket; the petunias add excitement while they establish the base from which the apple blossoms rise.

base; standing Oriental containers; low Oriental containers; polished-wood burls; baskets; handled containers; and urns.

Compotes are wide-topped vases with thick, occasionally ornate pedestals. They are predominantly used in traditional arrangements that display circles, triangles, and the Hogarth-curve designs.

Cylindrical vases are required for all vertical arrangements, whether Oriental, contemporary, or traditional. You should have these versatile containers on hand in a variety of colors and styles for use with snapdragons, larkspur, gladiolus, fruit blossoms, and many other flowers.

Shallow, oval bowls are indispensable to horizontal arrangements and to some Oriental and modern, triangular designs featuring round flowers, such as magnolias and Fuji mums. Shallow bowls with an attached base are most often employed in modern designs. They are superbly effective for displaying the sweeping curves of crescents, Orientals, asymmetrical triangles, and oval arrangements.

Tall, giant spikes of yellow snapdragons in a bright yellow vase immediately catch the eye. The bold vertical lines of the snapdragons require a tall container to create the proper proportion. The upward thrust of the yellow snapdragons and the vase is controlled, however, by the green-and-white wandering Jew leaves placed at the visual center of the arrangement, overhanging the container's edge. This foliage provides movement opposite that of the vase and the snapdragons, whose upward thrust would otherwise be too strong.

Deep bowls of all sizes and textures—from ceramic to enamel—blend with any style of floral design from a simple, round shape to an Oriental or high-tech modern arrangement. Deep bowls with attached bases are adaptable to traditional, modern, and Oriental design forms.

Standing Oriental containers, such as an ashtray on a base, are used in Oriental designs featuring large focal flowers. The sides of the ashtray will support the larger, focal flowers, such as magnolias and orchids, while the base will give the depth required for the style. Low Oriental containers, such as flat dishes with a slight lip, are ideal for Oriental designs in which wood and rock accessories are used. The wide open space of the dish allows for the careful placement required in ikebana designs.

Another container, the polished-wood burl, is essential to modern and Oriental designs and works extremely well in vegetative arrangements that reflect landscape scenes. Baskets of all textures, compositions, and shapes can be adapted to almost

53

Here, again, is an example of how much more prominent a role the container plays in an ikebana-inspired arrangement. The iridescent white glaze joins the white delphinium and the pink rubrum lilies. The vase also provides proportion, support, and fascinating contrast for the writhing, naked fruit branches. They twist away from the solidarity of the container, reaching for heaven.

A versatile arrangement composed of white flowers and a white container is a study in the contrast of textures. The basket, in this instance, is a part of the arrangement itself. The crinkly cosmos, waxy tulips, smooth irises, fluffy delphinium, and woven basket each contribute a different finish to the design. A few flashes of red in the tulips, holly, and centaury emphasize the brilliance of the white flowers and basket and their rich, interesting textures.

any design style though they are used most frequently in arrangements with a country motif. Because artificial flowers do not require water, you can experiment with a million design styles using innovative containers such as burls and baskets. It is difficult to hide a bulky water container for a real flower on a burl, but the stems of artificial flowers can be easily hidden from view. Baskets can hold only a limited amount of real flowers if they are to be effectively watered, while huge amounts of artificial flowers can overflow from a basket in a dramatic display.

Handled containers, such as teapots, coffeepots, cups, jugs, and pitchers—in pewter, copper, ceramic, and other materials—are striking and different. Always let some of the handle and spout show through your design to use the charm of the container most effectively.

Urns are stately and traditional, and are therefore seen most often in circular and triangular designs. Have them on hand in every size, texture, and color; you will find them useful

A continental triangle arrangement of pastel-colored flowers is superbly displayed in this long-necked container of pale pink ceramic. The long neck elevates the gorgeous arrangement to formal prominence and the bubble base reflects the burst of flowers above. A few purple and yellow cosmos, purple freesia, and other wildflowers are mixed with the pink elegantine to provide sufficient contrast so that the pink is not overwhelming.

because of their timeless popularity.

No discussion of containers would be complete without a description of the use and function of pedestals and bases. Historically, pedestals and bases were employed to protect furniture from scratches and spills, but today they provide professional finish. Large, mass arrangements, Oriental designs, and Hogarth-curve designs are almost always complemented by a tall pedestal that gives balance to the striking visual sweep of the arrangement.

Pedestals can be chosen to reflect the color of the flowers or to contrast or harmonize with the texture of the foliage. However, the pedestal should always be a supporting player, never dominating the arrangement. If the pedestal is not chosen carefully, the design will appear bottom-heavy. Lacquered wood, marble slabs, formal blocks, heavy metal stands, and Oriental mats are the bases used most often for arrangements. They are all simple, durable, and sturdy.

This listing merely covers the most basic and elemental container and

A regal silver bowl, usually the home for roses and orchids, is a marvelous container for a royal-colored arrangement of magnificent wildflowers. The refreshing juxtaposition of silver and wildflowers will surprise and intrigue the viewer. The pink liatris spikes, ruby-red freesia, purple wild larkspur, lavender sanguisorbas, pink buttercups, and white sweetpeas seem to "belong" in silver.

base needs. With each arrangement, seek out and discover an extra-special container that you know is perfect for the design you have in mind, the space it must fit into, and the effect you desire. Decidedly different lamp bases, unusual kitchen utensils, unique pieces of driftwood, magnificently shaped seashells, carved jewelry boxes, painted cake pans, copper tins, pewter egg cups, antique bottles, period soap dishes—a never-ending potpourri of ideas is available for you to experiment with. Searching for the right container can be a glorious adventure that takes you to antique shops and garage sales, into attics, basements, and secondhand stores. Look carefully for the perfect container that will make your display of flowers an integral jewel in your interior-design plan. Today, with the new freedom inherent in the employment of artificial flowers, the floral designer is on the threshold of creative, innovative floral design that is possible through the careful choosing and imaginative blend of artificial flowers and containers.

THE MECHANICS OF ARRANGING WITH ARTIFICIAL FLOWERS

The popularity of artificial floral design is due in part to the relative ease with which these flowers can be assembled in an arrangement. A designer can bend and shape them into position without worrying about damaging them. Also, these flowers are especially versatile because they do not require water or soil, eliminating spills and mess. Finally, any design can be disassembled quickly, and the flowers reused in other arrangements.

It is essential, however, to be familiar with the mechanics of arranging with artificial flowers before one can successfully assemble an artful design. The designer also must have certain tools and accessories on hand to complete an arrangement; these elements and their utilization are introduced and discussed in this chapter. Then, a number of simple strategies are offered to guarantee that the supporting picks, tape, foam, glue, and wire are camouflaged from view.

FLOWERS TO HAVE ON HAND

Every floral designer should have a ready supply of the most versatile artificial flowers. These flowers can be used in many different styles and designs, supporting more dramatic or spectacular blooms. Roses, carnations, dahlias, tulips, larkspur, lilacs, snapdragons, peonies, lilies, fruit-tree branches, anemones, Queen Anne's lace, and forget-me-nots are popular flowers that will complement myriad styles, though you will want to carefully choose the exact flowers for each new arrangement. The more of these basic flowers you have on hand, the more inspired your choices will be.

TOOLS AND SUPPLIES

A few helpful tools will make assembling your arrangements easier, as well as give them a professional, finished look. Suggested items include a lazy Susan, wire cutters, florist wire, floral picks, floral tape, floral foam, a razor knife or electric knife, and a glue gun.

The lazy Susan allows you to view your arrangement from all angles as you assemble it without the constant lifting and handling that is bothersome and can disrupt your design. Set the vase or container on the tray of the lazy Susan as you design the arrangement.

Most of the tools and accessories necessary for working with artificial flowers are pictured here. Clockwise from the top right: razor knife; scissors; wire cutters; glue sticks (for use in the hot glue gun); floral extenders; floral wire; hot glue gun; flowers and foliage; floral tape; basket with moss covering inside; natural tree branches; (in center) ceramic container with floral foam inside.

The next three photos demonstrate how to assemble a small apple tree with natural tree branches and artificial apple blossoms. The basic principles shown here can be adapted to the creation of any size tree.

Step 1:

The real fruit branches have been stripped of foliage and secured in the container in plaster of paris. The top of the container is covered with floral moss to hide the plaster of paris base. Holes are then drilled into, but not through, the branches at a downward angle with a ⅛-inch (30 millimeter) bit. Drill them wherever you would like to attach flowers or new branches.

A small pair of wire cutters will be very useful to cut and bend wire stems. Make sure that you obtain a pair that fits your hand comfortably and has a smooth-coated grip that won't irritate your skin. A good pair will also have a crimping feature that is essential for attaching metal floral picks to stems. Test the cutting and crimping features of several pair to see which is the most comfortable before you make your purchase.

FLORAL WIRE

The supporting stem for nearly every artificial flower is made of floral wire wrapped with floral tape. The most common gauge of floral wire used is #22, a size strong enough to support giant peonies, yet delicate enough for baby's breath and other tiny flowers. Have a roll on hand for repairs and to reinforce stems, if necessary.

FLORAL TAPE

Artificial flowers are usually purchased with attached wire stems covered with floral tape. However, at times you may need to cover the wire yourself, or you may decide to change the color of the tape to fit an arrangement's color scheme. Today, floral tape is available in green, red, pink, yellow, purple, blue, orange, white, brown and black—almost any color required for decorative coordination. Green floral tape, which most closely reflects nature's own color scheme, is of course the most popular and useful tape, so have a roll on hand. But why not pick up a roll or two in unusual colors so you can exploit the whimsical freedom of design that makes artificial flowers so exciting. Weddings, special themes, and seasonal arrangements, all of which embrace a particular color scheme, will be that much more dramatic with matching stems. Carry the pastels of a spring arrangement down into the vase, or emphasize the lovely red and green of a Christmas display by alternating the two colors on the stems of the featured flowers and branches.

Floral tape is available in one-half-inch (thirteen-millimeter) and one-inch (twenty-five-millimeter) widths, although the one-half-inch (thirteen-millimeter) width is easier to work with and won't bunch up awkwardly as the wider tape sometimes does. To wrap a stem wire with floral tape, begin under the blossom where the wire is attached. Wrap the tape

Step 2:
Attach a stem to each solitary blossom, or gather several blossoms on one end, if you would like. The blossoms are secured to the branch in two ways. The first method is to use a hot glue gun to shoot some glue into the drilled hole. Insert the stem of the blossom into the glue-filled hole. After the glue has dried, wrap floral tape of an appropriate color at the graft to disguise the joints. The other method, used where the branches are not thick enough for holes or to attach flowers where you have not drilled holes, is to lay the wire stem along the branches, then wrap it with floral tape.

around this part once or twice to secure the tape. Then hold the blossom in one hand and the tape in the other. Stretch the tape out and twist the stem into the stretched tape at an angle spiraling down until the stem is covered. Stretching the tape gives a clean, even finish to the stem. Cut the tape at the end and twist the excess around the stem to make sure it is secure. This whole procedure may take a little practice at first, but it will soon become second nature to you.

FLORAL PICKS

Once you have learned to wrap a stem, you can easily attach a floral pick, extend a stem length with new wire, and even create new blossom heads. Floral picks are used to lengthen and support stems, as well as to help to position the flower in floral foam.

The picks have one pointed end, which makes it easier to push into the foam. They are available from one to three inches (twenty-five to seventy-five millimeters) in length.

Floral picks were once made of wood and were cumbersome to handle. Today, they come in aluminum or another pliable metal and are easy to crimp. Take the end of your stem and set it so that about an inch (twenty-five millimeters) overlaps with the blunt end of the pick. This blunt end is curved and will partially wrap around the stem. Wrap the crimped portion with floral tape.

Many beginning arrangers want to attach floral picks to strengthen every stem, but this is not necessary. Instead, double the end of your stem by bending about an inch (twenty-five millimeters) of it back and wrapping this butt end with floral tape. This method is successful in arrangements where the containers will allow the flowers to stand on their own, not in foam, such as in a marble-filled container.

Often, you may need to extend the stem length of a flower to give it added height. Do this by cutting a piece of wire the exact length you wish the total stem to be. Place the cut wire next to the already existing stem. Securely wrap the two stems together with floral tape from the underside of the blossom, then all the way down the stem, stretching the tape and twisting the stem.

Using this same technique, many artificial floral designers combine single blooms together on one stem to

Step 3:
Place the larger blossoms toward the bottom of the tree
and the smaller blossoms at the top, simulating natural
growth.

It is not hard to wrap a stem with floral tape, especially after the stretching-and-twisting motion is mastered. Here, a stem is being strengthened with a floral pick. Lay the pick along the existing stem, then wrap it with tape, stretching the tape while twisting the stem. Cut the tape after the pick is wrapped to make sure there is enough tape to completely cover the stem.

give the impression of a multiheaded flower. For instance, wrap three dahlia blossoms to create a stunning flower that previously did not exist in nature! You also can combine several different-colored blooms of the same species on one stem, or even several different species on one stem for a spectacular effect.

FLORAL FOAM

Floral foam is used to hold the flower stems securely in position within an arrangement. Floral foam is usually needed when the container you are using has a wide neck, making it difficult to hold the flowers in place. The size and shape of the piece of floral foam you will need depends primarily on the size of the container you have picked. For instance, a shallow dish will take a relatively thin, square, or oblong piece of foam that allows you to use the whole surface of the container in your arrangement. A conical vase will require a smaller block that fits snugly near the bottom of the vase. In each case, you will want to use the minimum amount of foam necessary to hold the flowers securely in place.

Foam can be cut with a sharp razor

knife or with an electric knife if your hand is not steady. Cut the foam to fit tightly within the container, or secure it with a hot glue gun, available at artificial-flower markets and household-supply or art-supply stores. This gun is easy to use and will save you from having to deal with the other glues, pastes, plaster, putty, and adhesive tapes previously used for this job. The gun is loaded with a glue cartridge, which will be melted by a heat element in the gun. Press the trigger to release a few drops of glue. To secure your floral foam, shoot some hot glue into the container—four to ten drops, depending on the size of the vase—and then shoot a few drops onto the base of the foam. Place the foam glue side down in the container. The glue will dry in a few moments, and the foam will be safely secured.

Floral foam secured with a glue gun is most appropriate for containers where the foam will not be visible. However, you can use floral foam in a clear container. Cut a smaller piece of foam so there is space around it in the container. Secure it by putting marbles, wood chips, or stones around it. This will hide the foam and create an interesting effect as well.

FINISHING TOUCHES

Once the floral foam is secure, decide on the covering you will use to conceal the foam from view. Artificial moss, crushed rock, colored-glass pieces, marbles, and wood chips can be spread over the top of the floral foam and used to fill any spaces left between the foam and the container before you arrange the flowers.

Flowers will seem to grow naturally from moss or wood chips in a country or traditional arrangement. Moss is available on a roll; your floral market will sell you the size piece you require. When using artificial moss, cut a piece that is slightly larger than the opening of the container. Place it on top of the floral foam and tuck the ends into the container with your finger. When you insert the floral stems through the moss and into the foam, you will secure the moss as well. In some arrangements, you may position foliage and filler material close to the container; this may sufficiently camouflage the foam. If leaves and greenery are a part of your design, position them after the line and focal flowers are set, making sure they obscure the foam. Use the lazy Susan to check the arrangement from all angles for any bare spots where foam is exposed to the viewer.

Set your flowers firmly in place by pushing the stem all the way through the foam, to the bottom of the container. This will insure proper anchoring. If you are using a container filled with marbles, wood chips, or glass pieces, insert the stem in the same manner, to the bottom of the container. The marbles and chips will be sufficient to anchor the stem securely only if the stem is pushed through to the bottom.

It does not take much experience to become practiced in the mechanics of arranging. In the meantime, almost any mistake can be easily and quickly rectified when you are using artificial flowers. If a stem is cut too short, add some stem wire and restore the length. Or, if you don't like the results of an arrangement, dismantle it without wasting any materials and start again. Practice the mechanics by constructing small arrangements with a minimal number of elements—floral and mechanical—and your confidence will soar. As a result, your daring and creative inventiveness will guarantee you success and the admiration of all who view your work.

THE CARE AND CLEANING
OF ARTIFICIAL FLOWERS

The immortal beauty and increasingly sophisticated style of artificial flowers is in part achieved because they are composed from specially textured polyester. This fabric has been designed expressly to capture the brilliant colors of living blooms. It also allows the astonishingly close replication of the fabulous textures and subtle variations of real flowers. Finely patterned, delicate flower and leaf designs are printed directly on the richly textured fabric for a shockingly natural effect. This ingenious printing also ensures that the flowers' colors will never "bleed" in moisture or heat, as lesser-quality blooms may. The colors will not fade, either.

There are numerous delightful, practical features that have endeared these high-quality artificial flowers to designers all over the world. The easy-care characteristics of this polyester makes maintenance of arrangements, flowers, and trees virtually nonexistent. It is super-durable—nearly indestructible—and able to withstand rough treatment, including vigorous shakes, accidental spills, or yanks and pulls by playful children or overactive pets.

Furthermore, the fabric of these flowers is woven in a "crisscrossed" fiber texture that is remarkably dust-repellent. It is unnecessary for the owner of high-quality polyester plants to toil laboriously to keep the leaves and blooms of these flowers clean. Artificial flowers of lesser quality and believability, on the other hand, are usually constructed from a smooth-textured fabric that seems to attract dust like a magnet.

CLEANING PROCEDURES

Your artificial flowers will need to be cleaned periodically but this procedure is simple and will take very little time. Dust is removed by gently shaking the flower, or by passing a blow-dryer over the blossoms, leaves, and stems. With the dryer set on the low-cool position, work your way from the inside of the flower to the outside. This method will effortlessly take care of almost all your cleaning problems.

Although it is rare, some dust may lodge in the crisscrossed fabric fibers. To remove it, you will need a clear plastic bag and a half-teaspoon of table salt. Put the salt in the bag, then put the bloom in the bottom. Gather the bag around the stem and shake it gently for a few seconds. The salt will dislodge any dust imbedded in the fabric thoroughly and immediately.

If, for some reason, a flower or leaf does get soiled, quality artificial flowers can be gently hand-washed in cold water with a fine fabric soap, such as Woolite. Be careful that the stems, which are usually hand-wrapped, do not receive too much water. The flower can be hung to air-dry, or you can blow-dry it.

Make sure to check the fiber content of all flowers when you purchase them. A few varieties of artificial wildflowers are made of cotton and should be cleaned with a little extra care. Let them air-dry when you have washed them.

Artificial trees are cleverly designed so that most of the flowers, leaves, and branches are removable. Ask the salesperson to show you how this is done. Once disassembled, use the same, simple cleaning techniques and methods that you would use for artificial flowers.

OTHER CARE CONSIDERATIONS

Sunlight and artificial light have ruined many elegant, expensive, and elaborate natural flower arrangements because the blooms have

A poinsettia bloom or any other flower that has lost its shape can be easily revived in a few moments. Place the bloom on a soft cloth, and then lightly iron each petal with an iron set on warm. Do not use the steam setting because this will flatten the petals into an unnatural shape. The warm setting will return the shape, but leave enough wrinkle to give the petal natural texture.

If one of your artificial flowers becomes soiled, do not discard it. It is easy to restore its luster with a gentle washing. Fill a bowl with cold water and a capful of fine fabric detergent, such as Woolite. Gently swish the soiled flower in the soap mixture until the stain is removed. Now, swish the blossom in clear water to wash away the soap. Dry the flower by hanging it, patting it with paper towels, or blowing it with a hair dryer set on low. Note: Be careful to keep the stems from getting too wet; they might unravel if they are exposed to too much water.

"turned toward the light" or buds have opened prematurely, destroying the creative achievement. A magnificent arrangement of artificial flowers, however, will never twist and stretch toward light, and the petite, carefully placed buds will not open. The spirit of constant regeneration will be kept intact, and light, with all its shades and meanings, will become an interesting and thrilling accessory as never before employed.

Heat has also been the bane of floral design, but various types of heat—oil, steam, wood, coal, hot air—and air-conditioning have no effect whatsoever on these superb blooms and hearty foliage. Consequently, there is no wilting, sagging, or drooping, and arrangements can adorn spaces previously too close to a heat source or air-conditioning unit to sustain life.

Another benefit of artificial arrangements is that there is no need to change dirty, slimy water, wash filthy containers, or mess with dirt or chemicals. These flowers will look vibrant and alive no matter how little attention you pay to them.

The hazards of allergies are also eliminated because artificial flowers are nonallergenic. A person who has avoided roses for years because he or she is painfully allergic can now luxuriate without a care or worry in the splendor of dozens of gorgeous, artificial roses. And artificial flowers do not attract insects of any kind.

Many people are conditioned to the fragility of real flowers and, consequently, are afraid of damaging artificial flowers by handling them. Please remember that although they are superbly crafted to resemble real flowers in all aspects, they are also designed to be handled and touched. You will need to touch and feel them when you are planning arrangements and coordinating textures, or just to remind yourself that they are not real. The durability of these lifelike blooms, buds, and foliage is one of their most miraculous, unique, and appealing qualities, created for your enjoyment. Arrange them innovatively with a hands-on attitude.

INCORPORATING NATURAL FLOWERS

Every artificial floral arrangement faces the danger of becoming stale and boring through benign neglect. Many home designers have labored to create a magnificent arrangement with expensive artificial flowers and foliage; then, because it requires almost no care, they leave it for months or even years on end. The arrangement strays from its original eye-catching decorative purpose, and becomes "just another overworked piece of the furniture."

Avoid flat and neglected arrangements and create a unique, ever-changing sensation by periodically incorporating real flowers and foliage into your designs. Alter the patterns, textures, and colors slightly with different flowers, and keep your arrangements interesting and refreshed. By careful evaluation of the arrangement and what it needs to be revived, and the deliberate selection and positioning of just a few fresh flowers into the design, you can create a completely new and revitalized look with a minimum of effort and cost.

DECIDING ON NATURAL FLOWERS

The first step is to study your arrangement to determine what can be altered and which artificial blooms can be removed and most effectively replaced with fresh flowers. However, do not discard any artificial pieces; they can be cleaned and reused in another arrangement. Next, decide how much you would like to spend on fresh flowers, either weekly or for a special occasion. Then visit your local florist to see what is within your budget and available at the particular time of the year that you are shopping. You may choose a bouquet of daisies to distribute throughout your arrangement or you may decide to splurge on two or three expensive but stunning irises.

As mentioned in Chapter Five, "The Mechanics of Arranging," (see page 58), it is a good idea for the home designer to keep a base supply of the most versatile artificial flowers on hand. Irises, freesias, tulips, snapdragons, peonies, roses, forget-me-

Using natural flowers in an arrangement of artificial flowers requires special care—water can damage the artificial flowers. Here, a floral pincushion is placed in a shallow glass dish, then set into a simple black container, which is often used as the basis for Oriental designs. This dish will hold water for the fresh flowers, but it is best to add the water after the arrangement is completed. The glass dish is surrounded by clear marbles. The stems of three artificial gloxinia leaves and a branch of artificial orchids are pushed into the marbles, secure in their position but safely away from the water in the glass dish.

Two graceful, real calla lilies are now positioned in the pincushion. Before water is added, adjust the gloxinia leaves, orchids, and marbles to ensure the pincushion is completely obscured. Do this before water is added because it spills too easily when disturbed. Finally, use a turkey baster to add water to the dish.

nots, buttercups, wildflowers, maidenhair, and fruit-tree foliage are the most versatile flowers that can be adapted to almost any style and design, so these should be artificial. From this base of artificial flowers you can create three basic arrangements that you can add to and change periodically with fresh flowers. Irises, tulips, and snapdragons are a marvelous spring selection; add several pieces of real larkspur to enhance the color scheme yet keep in tune with the seasonal theme. Peonies, roses, and freesias are a midsummer selection that will be spectacular when you mix in some stunning, natural orchids, elevating the theme to a classic and elegant summer arrangement of regal flowers. Mix forget-me-nots, buttercups, maidenhair, and fruit-tree foliage with a blend of real wildflowers for a field arrangement. This bouquet can be altered to feature any of the seasons by changing the field flowers every few months.

Depending on the season, an inexpensive "supermarket bunch" of real

Now, a mass of pastel pink and yellow alstroemeria is tightly clustered at the center of the arrangement. The stems are secured in floral foam in a long, narrow dish set in the middle of the container; the fresh stems are positioned around the dish in water. The mass of fluffy alstroemeria provides a stunning contrast to the darker-colored, smooth-textured tulips.

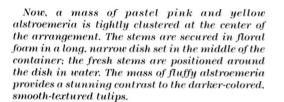

◀ *A general rule for mixing natural and artificial flowers is to first arrange the flowers of which there will be the most. Here, numerous fresh tulips are positioned to form a circle around the container. They establish the general shape of the arrangement, and their freshness is highlighted by their natural drooping form.*

flowers usually includes yellow-and-purple pansies, white daisies, and multicolored carnations. Buy one each week and intersperse the different flowers throughout your three basic artificial arrangements for new tones and textures constantly. Don't stick to the classic rules of which flowers go with which. Use your imagination and experiment with different combinations.

It is, of course, most economical to use striking artificial flowers and to incorporate real foliage, such as ferns and palms, fruit-tree branches, pussy willows, and berry branches. Much foliage can be found for free in your yard or nearby woods and fields. Foliage lasts longer than the real flowers, so you can change your combinations from week to week for refreshing looks.

WATER

When real flowers and foliage are included in an arrangement, they must be placed in water. Don't be afraid to place the artificial flowers in water

This country bouquet of artificial flowers could easily stand on its own. The mass of tulips, ranunculus, scabiosas, hyacinth, and orchids makes a perfect "base" arrangement. Real flowers can be added and changed for differing looks that reflect seasonal changes or special occasions. ▶

Here, fresh orange and white star of Bethlehem and fresh yellow roses are added to give the country bouquet a contemporary profile. The star of Bethlehem reach beyond the original perimeter of the arrangement, and the roses enhance the sunny yellow color. At another time, deep orange gerbera daisies could be added to highlight the burnt orange of the ranunculus. ▼

also. The floral tape on the stems will eventually disintegrate, but you can easily rewrap the wire stems with new tape. This approach will allow you to be very innovative in dealing with water and to let the mechanics enhance the design. For instance, if you are using a clear container, fill it with clear marbles. The marbles will support the real and artificial blooms that you position in the container. When you fill the container with water, the reflection of light sparkling through the marbles will be dazzling.

You can also make water an element of the design by adding food coloring. For example, if your design features real pink flowers and artificial green foliage, place them in a clear container with clear marbles and add water and red food coloring for an original effect. Let the water help to carry through the design scheme.

In shallow bowls and horizontal designs, use a floral oasis to hold flowers in place and provide water for the real blossoms. The oasis is secured in the container, and the flower stems are pushed through for anchoring. The oasis holds water like a sponge, nurturing the real flowers. At the same time, the artificial blooms will also be held in place by the oasis.

In some arrangements, you may choose to keep your artificial flowers out of the water. This can be done easily. First place a small glass or vial in the center of the container or in the area that will employ real flowers. Anchor the glass and hide it by surrounding it with chips of stone, marbles, or floral foam in the container. Any of these will also allow you to secure your artificial blooms. Position your flowers as you please, though you will have less flexibility with the real blossoms. Fill only the glass or vial with water.

No matter which method you use (and you will have to decide with every arrangement of real and artificial flowers which is the most effective), let the mechanics play an integral part and create a unique look in your arrangement.

SUGGESTIONS FOR MIXING REAL AND ARTIFICIAL FLOWERS

Through the creative employment of real flowers, you can change the color and style of any arrangement, usher in seasonal changes, and create distinctive Oriental designs. Some simple ideas are offered here, but you will probably want to improvise by using your favorite flowers or whatever is seasonally available.

Color Changes

An all-blue display of larkspur, grape hyacinth, and irises can be transformed instantly into a sparkling, warm arrangement with the simple addition of a few fresh yellow freesias or white narcissus. Any monochromatic design should be enlivened with color every once in a while, or you will tire of it. You can always return to the original monochromatic display for a time, but try using some real larkspur for a fresh touch. Add drama to an arrangement of zinnias, lilies, and roses in soft pastel shades by adding some real deep red roses and bright yellow irises.

Style Enhancement

Enhance a romantic arrangement of pink carnations and red freesias by adding a few real gladiolus. The gladiolus will bring another texture and hue to the arrangement, as well as

A crystal vase is filled with fresh star of Bethlehem, miniature carnations, gladiolus buds, and some twisting branches. This arrangement emphasizes their freshness, making them look as if they had just been picked from the garden. The stems of the natural flowers are left long so they can be pushed deeply into the water in the vase.

The appearance of this simple arrangement of freshly picked flowers is filled out with a few artificial flowers. Alstroemeria, freesia, and scabiosas are common garden flowers with unusual textures that will add contrast to this arrangement of similarly colored flowers. The stems of the artificial flowers are kept short so they can be secured within the cluster of fresh flower stems at the mouth of the vase, above the water.

A simple white, triangular arrangement, featuring three giant poinsettia blossoms, originates with the placement of the artificial blooms in a slender crystal bud vase. Large blossoms such as these are not usually displayed in a delicate vase, but the striking shape of the design makes the variation new and exciting.

change the shape of the design. The result will be a fuller, more romantic arrangement because the gladiolus will reach out and pull the viewer into the warmth of the display. Any style, whether romantic, Victorian, period, or contemporary, can easily be amended, enhanced, and refreshed by the simple addition of fresh flowers. They will add drama and contrast, and slightly alter the original intent of the arrangement.

Seasonal Changes

As the seasons change, a new variety of fresh flowers and foliage emerge. Add these to your arrangements to reflect the passage of time. Fresh summer roses will warm a spring Victorian arrangement, and spring lilies will defrost a winter greenery arrangement. In the autumn, incorporate the stunning beauty of nature's own colors by using leaf and berry branches in your arrangements. Mix yellow, white, and orange artificial Michaelmas daisies with real firethorn berry or holly berry branches. Take artificial marigolds, cornflowers, black-eyed Susans, and nasturtiums and arrange them with some spectacularly vivid leaf foliage for a wonderful autumn display.

Oriental Designs

Simple Oriental designs are perfect to employ both artificial and real flowers together. You can enhance the heaven-man-earth symbolism of the design by dramatically showing contrast and harmony together—harmony of design and the contrast of real and artificial flowers. Use three real irises along with three artificial, barren fruit-tree branches for a classic ikebana design that will startle you with its simple, graceful beauty.

These are just a few suggestions and ideas to encourage you to be creative with real flowers while remaining practical and economical. For many home floral designers, the joy of mixing real and artificial flowers in unusual ways has resulted in new definitions of real and artificial floral art that combine the best of both worlds.

Fresh white daisies now fill the empty space between the poinsettias and continue the white color scheme. A few sprays of pine provide an enlivening color backdrop for the drama of the poinsettia shapes. The pine sprays also contribute a needed contrast in texture.

STEP-BY-STEP DESIGNS

———

Here are several step-by-step arrangements that will enable you to visualize the basic elements, principles, and mechanics of artificial floral design. You'll see how the guidelines discussed in Chapter Five are employed to ensure the most appropriate, effective, and beautiful arrangement for any setting or situation.

This three-step spring display illustrates how a simple circular design can be beautifully expanded by contemporary lines that reach beyond established perimeters.

Step 1:

Begin by carefully selecting components in the arrangement so they complement each other perfectly. The straight, spiked lines of the white larkspur will contrast dramatically with the cascading flow of the lavender wisteria. The narrow-necked ceramic container will be almost hidden from view within the completed arrangement, but its bright yellow will echo the wisteria centers. It is also important to choose a container that is heavy enough to support the actual and visual weight of the chosen flowers.

When designing the arrangement, start by establishing the circular shape. Place the white larkspur in the container in a radiating form. The tallest larkspur is positioned at a height almost two-and-a-half times that of the container to correctly balance the arrangement.

Step 2:

Insert filler foliage near the floral base, and position downward to complete the circular shape.

Step 3:

Carefully place more green foliage to fill in the empty space within the circle and accent the outward movement of the white larkspur, which appears to burst out of the foliage in a dramatic explosion. For a final touch of contrast, insert some trailing, lavender wisteria at the base, continuing the downward flow of floral lines in all directions.

③

Step 1:
Secure floral foam in container, and cover it with sheet moss. Position the Michaelmas daisies in a free-flowing pattern with the largest blooms at the center and top of the arrangement.

Step 2:
Empty space is now filled in with greenery to enhance the skeletal shape of the display. The green foliage is a natural background for the white-and-yellow daisies.

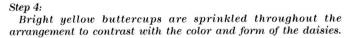

Step 3:
Some tiny daisies and forget-me-nots are set around the mossy base next, to elaborate on the natural theme of the arrangement.

Step 4:
Bright yellow buttercups are sprinkled throughout the arrangement to contrast with the color and form of the daisies.

Step 5:
Next, forget-me-nots are scattered throughout the arrangement in clusters of pastel blue and purple. Their cool color softens the daisies and the buttercups and adds another rich, harmonious color to the arrangement. A few bare fruit branches, reaching upward, establish the proper height of the arrangement and add the promise of "blooms yet to come." The finished arrangement reflects the complete harmony within a natural setting.

5

Step 1:
    An interesting blend of greens and yellows gives this classical arrangement a contemporary flair. The focal dahlias and buds are placed securely in the container in a radiating skeletal framework.

Step 2:
    Next, Queen Anne's lace are added to fill in and strengthen the form. One blossom is positioned higher in the arrangement to assure correct proportion. The creamy colors of the dahlias and the lace have a warming effect on the viewer.

Step 3:
    Next, wandering Jew leaves are placed at the floral base of the arrangement. The interesting lines of these leaves create visual movement in the design. The eye wanders around the arrangement, then is brought back to the wandering Jew leaves to begin the circular journey again.

Step 4:
    Finally, to unify and blend the arrangement, a few spindle leaves are added to the lower left and top of the arrangement. The cooling dark green and white of these leaves help to set the perimeter of the design, and the texture of the leaves is complementary to the creamy color of the flowers. The overall effect is a warm arrangement of contrasting greens and yellows.

4

Step 1:
  Each step of this arrangement creates a different accent for the focal pink rubrum lilies. The lilies are placed in the arrangement first, establishing the height of the design. The color of the lilies is harmonized with the pink ceramic container, which establishes weight and balance in the reaching lilies.

Step 2:
  Dracaena leaves placed to the left side of the lilies build an asymmetrical triangle shape. They also create a contrast to further emphasize the preeminence and lift of the lilies.

Step 3:
  Next, smaller white lilies are incorporated to echo and frame the pink lilies. Their cheeriness lightens the overall look of the design.

Step 4:
  Finally, white camellias and buds complete the balance and add to the romantic effect. The pink lilies seem suspended in the air like shining stars.

Step 1:
Striking dramatic colors are the key to this ikebana-inspired design. The vertical line of the arrangement is established by setting the giant, red alstroemeria in place. The shallow black dish gives the arrangement bottom weight so that the reaching alstroemeria does not seem precariously positioned.

Step 2:
Next, medium-sized pink alstroemeria fill out the arrangement. Their colors softly contrast with the red, gently toning down the hot color.

Step 3:
Three light pink clematis are set at different heights in the lower left corner of the arrangement, reflecting the earth-man-heaven symbolism of ikebana floral design. This burst of light pink also tones down the hot red alstroemeria and adds to the cascading effect of the flowers.

Step 4:
Three deep green leaves are placed in a fan shape at the base of the bouquet to fill the empty space remaining and to add rich lushness. The finished arrangement now looks like a floral waterfall, with the flowers flowing downward in a stream of tropical color.

NATURALIZING EFFECTS—SCENTING

The final touch guaranteed to add authenticity to artificial floral displays is the "scenting" of your arrangement. Although this is an option, the wide variety of natural oils, potpourri, fragrant waters, spices, herbs, and extracts now available allows the designer of artificial floral displays to enhance the flowers with luscious aromas that will linger in the air and tantalize anyone who enters the room. The already surprising beauty of artificial flowers can be further dramatized by scenting your arrangement with essences of your personal choice in unusual and unexpected combinations.

Today, scents are readily available, easy to use and store, and, when purchased in nontoxic form, are safe to employ around children and pets. A work area in your garage or basement will be the perfect place for your floral laboratory. Follow the suggested guidelines below, but feel free to experiment with your favorite scents.

NATURAL OILS

Flower-Oil Essences

The essences of hundreds of flowers are available as oils sold in tiny vials in department stores, beauty shops, natural-food stores, and Oriental gift shops. The most popular and well-known oils include sweet-smelling rose, refreshing lilac, gentle lily of the valley, exotic lotus, spicy jasmine, mysterious frangipani, enchanting heliotrope, and woodsy French tuberose. Purchase a wide variety of essences to have on hand for any display you create, or any whimsical mix you desire.

Fruit-Oil Essences

Although not as popular as flower essences, fruit essences create an astonishing effect when applied to artificial flowers. Orange, pineapple, lemon, and lime are tropical scents that are wonderful when used for arrangements in the kitchen and on the patio. There, light-colored flowers and abundant greenery "bring the outdoors in" even more effectively when assisted by a tropical scent that suggests sunshine and fresh fruit. Strawberry, cherry, apple, and raspberry provide a country scent reminiscent of ripe orchards, golden fields, and romantic brambles. These fragrances are wonderful, especially in midwinter, for imparting a warm, welcoming feeling to your arrangements and your home.

Use of Oils

The only tools required to scent flowers with fragrance oils are an atomizer and an eyedropper. An atomizer is most effective because you can scent a much broader area with it than you can with just an eyedropper. Any empty perfume bottle will be perfect for use as an atomizer. Use the eyedropper to fill it after the previous scent has been completely rinsed away.

With the eyedropper, measure four parts oil to one part household alcohol into the atomizer. Secure the top to the atomizer tightly, then shake vigorously for a few seconds. The alcohol will dilute the oil, which is necessary because some oils used at full strength will stain the fabric of the flowers. You will probably smell the alcohol for a few seconds, but it will evaporate quickly and the natural scent will come forth, gradually without overpowering you. Take the atomizer and spritz the arrangement generously, especially on the leaves and the underside of the flowers, without worry of staining, for the diluted solution will not leave any traces.

If you choose to use an eyedropper to scent your flowers, put a few drops of undiluted oil into the heart of each flower, where it will not be noticeable. Sniff to see if more scent is required. Remember that it is easy to add more scent if you want a stronger smell, but it is extremely difficult to remove scent that is displeasing and overwhelming. Always proceed with cau-

Here, a giant white peony is scented with an eyedropper filled with woodsy French tuberose oil. Note that a few drops of undiluted oil are dropped directly into the center of the flower. When using an eyedropper, squeeze only two drops at a time, then sniff to see if more scent is required.

tion, for these scents last for one to two weeks. If you overscent you will either have to live with it or disassemble your arrangement, wash each flower, and start again.

POTPOURRI

A very safe and effective method for scenting your arrangements is to use floral and spice potpourri. Potpourri is a mixture of dried flowers, seed heads, fruit-rind pieces, and spices that retain their natural fragrances for long periods of time after being dried. The most popular potpourri mixtures include honeysuckle, rose, lilac, hyacinth, lavender, freesia, violet, lily of the valley, clove, pine, orange, apple, lemon, and lime. Potpourri is amazingly longlasting; it will release its fragrance with renewed vigor every time it is stirred or shifted and a new surface is exposed to the air. For this reason, potpourri is perfect to keep the somewhat permanent artificial arrangement smelling wonderful and fresh.

Today, potpourri is available in a wide variety of traditional mixtures and exotic combinations from around the world. To use potpourri, spread a thick carpet of it at the base of your arrangement, on top of any floral moss if there is room for it. If there is

little room in your arrangement, just put some potpourri in a small, interesting bowl and set it next to the floral display for the same effect. This will also allow you the flexibility to change the fragrance as you wish by replacing the bowl full of potpourri with one of another mix. Potpourri ingredients can be purchased individually and mixed at home in minutes for personally designed fragrance combinations.

FRAGRANT WATERS

Fragrant waters have been used for centuries to scent a variety of objects from furniture to hair. Rose water, the most popular, is sister to the sweet-smelling waters made from the petals of the orange blossom, lilac, and lily of the valley. These popular fragrant waters are conveniently available in all markets and are easily applied to arrangements. There is no mixing and no worry of staining because the waters are sold in a diluted form. Fill an atomizer with the fragrant water and spritz generously over your arrangement. Spray until the fragrance lingers in the air without overpowering the room. The desired effect is subtle, not overwhelming. The only disadvantage to using fragrant waters is that their effect is ephemeral, and

the fragrant smell will last for only a day per application.

SPICES AND HERBS

Almost every spice and herb has a fragrance that can be employed when scenting an arrangement. The floral designer will have to choose from hundreds of spices and herbs, but the most versatile spices and herbs are mint, tarragon, basil, rosemary, dill, cloves, and coriander.

Tarragon is woodsy and fresh, and very effective with all-green arrangements. It adds a delightful aroma to lotus blossoms. Basil, rosemary, and mint can be mixed together at Christmas and New Year's for scenting artificial evergreens with a pungent, fresh-picked smell. Dill is evocative of full harvests and preserving time and will bring the autumn season directly to your hearth. Cloves are popular for their unique scent and should be included in arrangements that feature fruit. Try cloves in a small floral arrangement placed on the bathroom window ledge for a comfortable "good morning" effect. Coriander has a faint, gingery fragrance that is pleasant in Oriental arrangements; it is a gentle partner in the heaven-man-earth symbolism of these designs.

All spices and herbs can be sprin-

kled lightly or in a thick carpet at the base of the arrangement. Use them on top of the floral moss, just as you would potpourri. However, spices and herbs are effective for only one or two days before their fragrance fades.

EXTRACTS

You will find dozens of cooking extracts of spices, herbs, fruits, and flowers in any supermarket. They can be used in the same way as essence oils with an atomizer or eyedropper. Extracts are best for a short-term effect because they are not as stable as essence oils. Extracts have varying amounts of alcohol in their composition, so you may need to add a little water to dilute the extract further. Try to locate extracts that do not contain corn syrup or sweeteners as this may attract insects to the arrangement. An unexpectedly interesting combination is vanilla extract sprayed on the leaves of white lilies or on the base of a homemade tree. Vanilla's sweet, tropical aroma will blend with the arrangements perfectly.

One final note of caution: commercial house-sprays and scent sticks that mimic floral and fruit fragrances are not recommended for floral scenting. Their chemical makeup is likely to damage the delicate dyes of the artificial flowers. Besides, they are designed to cover up unpleasant household odors and will cheapen and overwhelm your flowers instead of adding a light fragrance to the air.

Experiment with your favorite oils, potpourri, fragrant waters, herbs, spices, and extracts to create the scent you feel is correct for each individual arrangement and setting. Always remember to employ the scent modestly, so the viewer is not overwhelmed, but barely conscious that it is there.

An arrangement of climbing roses, wild roses, and forest hyacinth now only needs one final touch of reality—scent. A perfume atomizer is perfect for the job. Here, rose water is spritzed generously over the entire arrangement. The air is filled with a sweet lingering fragrance that will be immediately noticed by anyone entering the room.

INTERIOR DESIGN WITH ARTIFICIAL FLOWERS

ROOM-BY-ROOM DESIGNS

Each room in the home is decorated and designed to fulfill a specific purpose. The artificial floral arrangements can be used as a key design element to enhance and accentuate the unique role of each room. In addition, the interior design of a room is a reflection of the occupant's values, lifestyle, and personality, and the right floral display can provide the final touch to make the occupant and his or her guests feel right at home. A copper teakettle, for instance, filled with daisies and buttercups in the kitchen will offer a friendly hello. A spreading bougainvillea vine incorporated dramatically into a striking living room design can stimulate conversation and encourage social interaction. A dining room display of roses can change as the room's atmosphere changes by simply altering the container—formal for a special occasion or informal for a relaxed family gathering.

In any room, an artificial floral display can be used to accent a painting, complement a fabric pattern, contrast a wall color, and integrate chairs, sofas, tables, and other accessories into the overall design statement. The permanence of artificial flowers has made a special impact on interior design, for flowers now can be used deliberately and constantly in all kinds of ways, from the colorful centerpiece of a room's grand design to a toning accessory that works subtly.

The primary consideration in floral design for a room is restraint, an element that typifies the aesthetic success of Oriental design. An arrangement should always add to the room's style, not overwhelm it. Large, hodgepodge arrangements, even when displayed in beautiful, period containers, add nothing but confusion to a room. Carefully study the colors and style of the room and its furnishings, and the setting you have chosen for the display. Be sure to choose a container that is in perfect harmony with the room design. Keep these basics in mind as we discuss the various rooms in a home and how best to create arrangements for them.

The entrance hall of this home is brought to life with an Oriental arrangement featuring a giant red lotus. The earth tones of the wallpaper, area rug, lacquered Korean chest, and statue are warm and welcoming, yet they lack color and vitality. The red blossom adds excitement with a burst of color while three cream-colored orchids harmonize the arrangement with its surroundings. This simple arrangement fits perfectly between the mirror and the chest. If the design were any larger or more elaborate, it would overwhelm the small area where it is displayed.

THE ENTRANCE AND HALLWAY

The floral arrangement you choose to place in the hall or entrance is the initial welcoming symbol for your family and guests, and as such, should keynote your hospitality and warm invitation. Space is usually limited in this area, however, so the floral design must be simple and uncluttered, ensuring there will be no hazard of guests accidentally knocking over an arrangement as they remove their coats. Flowers placed here will also create a mood and atmosphere you want people to share. A single lotus blossom arranged with a few green leaves and placed in a wall alcove or on a shelf will convey peace and tranquillity to all who enter. Or seasonal themes are perfect for this area. Just a couple of bright yellow forsythia blossoms in a tall, narrow container will bring the freshness of spring into the entrance. If a mirror hangs in your hallway, place an arrangement in the sweeping lines of a Hogarth curve for a magnificent dis-

A cozy kitchen nook exudes the freshness of a country morning when a basket brimming with starburst daisies, yellow buttercups, and blue forget-me-nots is set upon the breakfast table. Carefully positioned to seem haphazardly placed, the wildflowers seem freshly picked. Their exciting colors and textures reflect nature's unadorned beauty.

play of formality and elegance that will foreshadow the feeling of the rest of the home.

The hall is also a dynamic location for miniature arrangements, such as a few tiny orchids or agapanthus displayed on a table next to an interesting accessory—a figurine, a small dish, or a shell. Whatever you do, remember to keep it simple, for you will want to change the design often, creating a fresh welcome.

THE KITCHEN

The kitchen is often the center of activity in a home. It is where the day begins, where a family gathers then and all through the day, and where informal conversation occurs as meals are prepared. The floral design you employ here must be versatile enough to harmonize with the many functions of this room, while always evoking a compatible mood.

A window over the sink is a marvelous place for a hanging plant—the colorful magnolia, for instance, or again, some trailing bougainvillea for

A table set for tea is carefully coordinated for a breathtaking effect. Here, the artificial roses in a pitcher, while outstanding for their rich red color, are part of the whole room's design, with each piece making a contribution of equal importance. The table has been set with Limoges china with a ribbon-and-bow pattern that matches the rosebud print on the tablecloth and napkins. Wallpaper featuring trellised wisteria is matched to the hanging lamp. A small shelf displays a raspberry Limoges plate and a small arrangement of ranunculus in many colors. The large pot of artificial ivy is the final touch of class in this "whole room design."

a tropical welcome with the morning sun and a cup of coffee or tea. Orange blossoms, cherry blossoms, and apple blossoms should be arranged in a window to add vitality and freshness to a dull view. A flowering climbing vine can be deliberately twisted around a window and over a cupboard, adding some outdoor naturalness to the room's informality.

Kitchen arrangements should reflect sunshine colors, such as yellow nasturtiums curving downward from a vase hung on a white wall, or orange marigolds in a copper kettle. It is also fun to use containers that echo the utilitarian purpose of the room, such as egg-holders, ladles, baskets, bowls, glasses, bottles, tureens, and pots. A few tiny roses in an antique bottle of colored glass will infuse any breakfast table with cheerfulness and beauty. Blend one or two hydrangea blossoms and a few green leaves into a bowl with seasonal fruits and vegetables for a spectacular, colorful centerpiece for table or countertop. In any case, the key to kitchen arrangements is warmth and informality, reflecting the room's function and atmosphere.

The soft, warm colors of this dining room require flowers that will enhance their elegance and relaxed tone. The centerpiece of pink and white roses and buds is luxurious, yet not so high and imposing that it will hinder conversation across the table. A large lavender rhododendron bush set in the corner blends well with the flowered drapes and does not overpower the room with its size. Bold colors in this setting would be improper, detracting from the calming, candlelit atmosphere created, where people and food are the most important features.

THE DINING ROOM

Today, the dining room is the setting for a variety of functions—formal dinners, casual family get-togethers, and neighborly coffee klatches and teas, club meetings, and planning sessions. The type of floral arrangement you will want to develop will be dictated by these specific functions. It is wise to create a simple centerpiece or arrangement that can be formalized with the addition of a few flowers and foliage. For example, the yellow chrysanthemums and green foliage that are normally displayed can be made more elegant for a special dinner or brunch by adding some lavender irises and white anemones. You should always have a small stock of popular flowers on hand to give you this flexibility.

Whatever the functions you need to fulfill, there are three rules you must always keep in mind when you design an arrangement to be displayed in the dining room.

RULE 1. No arrangement should be so large or dense that it obscures the view or blocks conversation across the table.

RULE 2. Because of the close scrutiny your arrangement will face from your guests at the table, the flowers should be perfect at all times, and the anchor must be well hidden.

RULE 3. Flowers in the dining room *should not* be scented, for they will clash with the flavors and aromas of the main attraction—the meal.

Dining tables are perfect for low, horizontal arrangements that extend outward to the sides of the table, and for smaller formal designs in round or triangular shapes. Sideboards and buffet tables can best display large arrangements or several small accent arrangements.

Some dining rooms have one central arrangement, keyed in color and period to the style of the room and displayed on the dining table or buffet, and several smaller complementary arrangements spread around the table and the room for a dramatic, unifying effect. Use a bouquet of grape hyacinths, roses, violets, and larkspur as your main arrangement, then set a bouquet of miniature violets in individual cups or tiny baskets at each place at the table. In the coordination of these several arrangements, you may choose to contrast the basic elements in the room, such as the draperies, but you can also try to do the whole room in monochromatic shades for a rich, textured effect. Linens, wallpaper, plate patterns, and flowers can be blended with tremendous variation of result.

Your dinnerware, tablecloth, placemats, napkins, candles, and containers can also be changed and rearranged to create differing atmospheres and effects. Lovely pink lotus blossoms are a perfect luncheon centerpiece, with white china plates and white linen napkins set on lotus-leaf placemats. For a small dinner party, keep the same pink lotus blossoms and lotus-leaf placemats, but use now deep green Majolica plates accompanied by linen napkins with a pink geranium-bud pattern on them.

This arrangement is evidence of the stunning impact a single bloom perfectly harmonized with a particular setting can have. The subtle beauty of the large white lotus blossom is not apparent immediately because the white flower is so complemented by the ceramic lamp and the Chinese screen. However, upon closer examination, this contemplative corner has an exotic, reflective aura that is imparted by the soothing serenity inherent in the lotus.

A huge display of larkspur, ranunculus, and bougainvillea set on a pedestal becomes an integral "piece of furniture" in this modern, eclectic family room. The arrangement's colors reflect the furniture and pillow fabrics, for harmony of color is the basis of the design. Although the arrangement is immense, it blends with its setting so it is not too overwhelming. Bolder colors would detract from the comfort of the room's casual atmosphere.

THE LIVING ROOM

The floral arrangements you put in the living room are the most important in your home. Here, they play a vital role in infusing simple home designs with the warmth and charm that is the essence of this room, the center of rest and relaxation for your friends and family. Living rooms generally have a fireplace with a mantel, a coffee table, smaller side tables, at least one large window, paintings and prints, and shelves—all spectacular settings for enhancing floral displays.

The mantel will be a main display center for the living room. It is stunning to feature twin arrangements, one on either end of the mantel. Triangular and curved arrangements fit beautifully centered between two candlesticks, and a fine painting or print hanging above the mantel can be complemented by a floral arrangement reflecting its colors and textures. For example, three Tokyo roses set just below an Oriental watercolor will attract the viewer's eye to the sweep and flow of the painting's color

It is not always necessary to make an extensive change in furniture or interior decoration to revitalize a room. Here, a simply decorated, comfortable living room is enlivened by a colorful arrangement set on a table in the center of the room. Magnolia blossoms, buttercups, and raspberries reach in all directions, orange nasturtium overflow the base, and ranunculus wander all through the arrangement. This display of movement in all directions at once awakens this pleasant but passive setting.

scheme without overwhelming it.

A table behind a couch is perfect for displaying a large, focal arrangement of stunning mass and color that will extend the boundaries of the room by becoming a piece of the furniture itself. The coffee table in front of the couch is ideal for a smaller mass arrangement accompanied by a few accessories, such as porcelain or glass figurines.

Living room windows, especially those with a seat, look magnificent with large baskets brimming over with blossoms in pastel colors—pale blues, pinks, pale purples—or strong flowers such as peonies placed to one side. A nonworking fireplace also is a superb place to display these colorful baskets.

If you have large, open spaces in your living room, you can define different areas with large foliage and long branches arranged for a dramatic line effect. Use a giant, self-made ficus tree to soften sharp architectural lines in a modern home. A large, high-ceilinged room with white walls and Spanish-tile floor was grace-

An informal arrangement set on a wicker chest at the foot of the bed brings the beauty of nature into a man's room. Hearty flowers in bold colors, such as red cosmos, brilliant African marigolds, and multicolored ranunculus and colchicum are arranged in a neutral-colored basket. The free spirit of the design is well-suited to the contemporary feel of the room. The warm analogous color scheme brightens even more against the dark green backdrop, but harmonizes with the light wood furniture as well.

fully brought down to size when a huge, green, areca palm tree in a giant wicker basket was placed next to another giant basket of fuchsia and lavender azalea in one corner of the room.

The living room is usually the only room large enough to carry oversized driftwood, large kettles, and giant containers of differing textures. Here, also, nature and the outside is invited into the home through the large windows. Some of your arrangements should take advantage of this and be bold and dramatic with stunning colors and interesting shapes. They should stimulate the viewer, as well as characterize the personality and atmosphere of your home and family.

THE BEDROOM

The right floral display in the bedroom can do a great deal to enhance the design scheme of the room. If a bedroom is Victorian in style, set two or three lovely miniature arrangements in period perfume bottles

*A woman's bedroom is warmed by an arrangement of flowers in soft, traditional "feminine" tones of
lavender, pink, and white. Pompon dahlias, ranunculus, wisteria, and alstroemeria are arranged in a
semi-formal manner appropriate to the room's decor and furniture style. The gentle flowers emphasize the
calm and gracious feeling of this room.*

Antiques often come alive when juxtaposed with a colorful, richly textured floral arrangement. This lovely wash-table-cum-dresser, cushioned chair, and lovely picture frame are magnificently revived by an invigorating contemporary floral design. A basket containing bright orange, red, and white daisies provides color and texture contrast. The smooth, beautifully crafted furniture pieces and the bright floral arrangement work to create excitement and vigor.

upon a dressing table. Geraniums, lilies of the valley, tiny anemones, and delicate roses look graceful on the dresser, next to a mirror, or on a chest at the foot of a bed where they will welcome you in the morning and suggest tranquillity to ease you to sleep.

Always make sure that the floral arrangements you design for the bedroom complement the style of the room. They should never compete for attention with the other elements of the room, but instead, should add a soft, subdued effect of peace and harmony through use of gentle colors and shapes.

THE BATHROOM

The bathroom is a delightful setting for small, cheerful arrangements that complement the color scheme, enliven textures and generally help to put you in a good mood as you prepare for the coming day. Small bottles, shaving mugs, boxes, tiny baskets, and soap dishes are wonderful when filled with small rosebuds, daisies, African violets, marigolds, and

Here is a spectacular sitting room in which every component is carefully coordinated. The upholstery fabrics and wall coverings are complementary and extend a cool, soothing invitation to relax on the comfortable wicker seats. Lavender wisteria hang lazily from the ceiling, almost connecting with a large spring arrangement of larkspur and alstroemeria that sits beside the furniture. The flowers were deliberately chosen for their calm, spring colors and to continue the room's total concept without overpowering it.

morning glories. Place bouquets at different levels on window sills, bathtub edges, toilet-tank tops, vanity tables, and hang them on the wall between towel holders. You should follow the color scheme but also include one or two vibrant blooms for an "eye-opening" effect.

THE SUNPORCH OR TERRACE

Informality is the key to sunporch and terrace arrangements. Here is where your home is closest to nature and the outdoors. Fill shells, baskets, and terra-cotta containers with wildflowers to bring fields and forests into the room, as well as the peaceful tranquillity of nature and a feeling of freedom. Display seasonal flowers and greens in bunches, unaffected, as they grow naturally. To dress up a terrace or porch for a brunch or early-evening meal, put tawny day lilies in a deep burnt orange glass container to recall a wakening sunrise or the glow of a spectacular sunset.

SEASONAL THEMES

Each season is defined by the flowers that blossom during that time. The vast variety of flowers will enable you to change your arrangements either slightly or dramatically for fresh, new looks. And with artificial flowers, out-of-season blooms can be mixed with seasonal blooms for surprising and innovative designs.

SPRING

Spring is the time of rebirth in nature. Your arrangements should reflect this natural phenomenon, so make them slightly less formal and stylized than during other seasons. The most prevalent colors in spring flowers include white, purple, yellow, and blue, so feature these colors abundantly in your designs. Crocuses and lilies of the valley are pushing their way up through the soft mosses growing beneath flowering trees, and this should be mirrored in your arrangements. Display lovely, blossoming branches of pink dogwood and pink and white mountain laurel alone in a wooden container for a spectacular effect. Or

dramatically infuse them with spring-time by adding a few lilies of the valley and crocuses at the base of the design.

An unusual tree stump outdoors is a fantastic spring container. Line it with moss and a few interesting stones, then fill it with tulips and greenery as if they are growing naturally out of the stump.

Spring Oriental arrangements would include quince and apple blossom branches carefully placed to emphasize each branch's line and blooms. Arrange some bright yellow daffodils between lime green Norwegian maple blossoms for a springtime show that unexpectedly but effectively mixes two totally different flowers and colors. Set a dark green bowl filled with huge, pink and white magnolia blossoms in a dark corner for a lightening effect traditional in Oriental homes.

Tulips and anemones come in the greatest variety of colors of any spring flowers. Mix blue and purple anemones with yellow and white daffodils and tulips, or pink anemones with

The rich tones of purple and yellow primula are displayed in a natural wicker rocking basket. Spring flowers are so fresh and their colors so brilliant that they should be massed in bunches and displayed throughout the home.

A lovely French country arrangement featuring the pastel colors of spring provides a continental welcome
in the entrance hall. The soft pink and white elegantine and the pink roses are smoothly complemented
by the sweetpeas, orchids, and starry forget-me-nots. The painted wicker container adds a distinctive
touch of elegant beauty to the overall visual harmony of this arrangement.

These wildflowers reflect the intense beauty and variety of textures available in summer's blooms. A contemporary triangular arrangement of white daisies, yellow buttercups and ranunculus, and purple wild larkspur and thistle sparkles like a pirate's chest of precious stones. Set in a white basket that enhances the color contrasts, this arrangement brings the essence of summer to any room in the house.

purple irises and yellow tulips, or red tulips with purple irises and white anemones to signify the explosion and reinvigoration of spring.

Carry the joy of spring into every room of your home. Start by arranging one massive display of lilies, tulips, anemones, daffodils, irises, crocuses, and spring roses in the living room. Then spotlight the individual component flowers in smaller arrangements throughout the house—a bouquet of irises in the kitchen, a cluster of tulips in the bedroom, and a graceful group of lilies in the bathroom.

SUMMER

Summer is the season when life is fullest and endowed with a bursting profusion of color, texture, and strong scent. You can bring summer into your home with mounds of brilliantly colored flowers, as well as with cooler soft pastels. But remember: The word to describe summer is abundance.

The living room should have an enormous basket displaying snapdragons, peonies, roses, larkspur, dahlias, lilacs, zinnias, and nasturtiums arranged in a breathtaking mass of color. As in springtime, set smaller arrangements of the same flowers in different areas of your home to carry through the vitality of this central arrangement.

Cool your home with arrangements that feature white flowers. Set them all around the house. A group of heavy, white, giant peonies, for example, cut short and accompanied by their own magnificent foliage is a wonderfully easy, informal summer design for the dining room. Formalize it for evening by adding a few pink peonies and reaching blue larkspur spikes.

All the varieties of lilies bloom in summer, and an arrangement of several types of lilies and buds with an abundance of foliage in a tall, green container will look impressive on your porch or in your kitchen. Tall gladiolus, also blooming in summer, displayed in a black vase are magnificent on a piano or small lamp table in a contemporary-style room.

Rambling roses are the flowers for every occasion and mood in summer.

This basket of spectacular yellow Michaelmas daisies captures the brilliant sunshine of summer. The round arrangement reflects the Flemish influence in floral design also indicated by the lemons. The mix of flowers and fruit symbolized to the Flemish the abundance of nature's most prolific season.

With the onset of cooler weather in early autumn, the floral palette becomes deeper in tone. A lovely basket of deep purple ranunculus, liatris, and thistle reflects this change. The beautiful bare branches emphasize how lovely this time of year can be. However, winter has not yet arrived, and the tawny ranunculus and wild hyacinth prove that there is plenty of life in this colorful time of the year.

Place cool pink-and-white bunches in the bedroom and bathroom. Use lively red roses in the living room and dining room, displayed in glass, crystal, or more formal silver containers. Field flowers and wildflowers are peaking in summer and every living room, kitchen, and porch should have at least one basket filled to the brim with Queen Anne's lace, buttercups, and varietal grasses for a country-meadow effect.

Since nature offers so many beautiful flowers to work with during this season, relax the rules of arranging a little and be daring, colorful and abundant in your displays.

AUTUMN

Autumn's display of foliage in richly mixed shades of orange, red-brown, and gold offers a final spectacular fling before the onset of winter. These colors often lend themselves well to home display because they complement wood furnishings and interior fabrics and enrich them.

Gather all the flowers that glow in varying shades of gold—chrysanthe-

This wildflower bouquet pays tribute to the rich, analogous colors of autumn. Soft orange ranunculus are crowned by burgundy ones, an imitation of the deepening of nature's color as winter approaches. The dark-colored wheat reminds the viewer of the bounty of this season. The delicate sprigs of flowering rush add a lighter color that reminds one of spring and that autumn is but one phase in a continuing cycle.

Winter's fruits and flowers are abundant in color and rich in texture. Mounds of white camellias are piled high in this display, along with red apples, pine cones, holly, and blackberries. Any room will be brightened and warmed by the winter's light of this breathtaking mix of fruits and flowers.

This creative winter arrangement can be assembled in minutes with poinsettia blossoms, pine branches, and holly. The fragile beauty of winter is reflected in the white poinsettia blooms set against the backdrop of hearty pine branches and holly leaves. The round, white ceramic container is as smooth as a carefully packed snowball.

mums, dahlias, marigolds, and trailing nasturtiums. Mix branches of copper beech and goldenrod together for a rich feeling of autumn's brilliance, reminding one of a beautiful sunset on a blustery day.

Live foliage from azalea and forsythia bushes can be added to your artificial dogwood and clematis for a vivid display of color. Change the live branches every few days as the tones of the leaves deepen, making every day a new adventure.

Dahlias, Michaelmas daisies, and forsythia greens are at their height in the autumn. Pull the red and pink daisies and dahlias from your summer arrangements and mix them with forsythia foliage in a glass container. Combine tangerine dahlias and green foliage in a white jug, and set it on the floor in the hall or living room. Marigolds are also seasonal in autumn. Display them throughout your home in clustered bunches of autumn colors in copper, pewter, and terra-cotta containers. Twist grapevines through the flowers and over the edges of the vase to remind you of a tramp through the woods on a crisp

autumn day.

Pumpkins, gourds, squashes, and Indian corn mixed with autumn berries and fruit branches evoke a colorful harvest theme. Live fruit, such as apples, pears, and artificial grapes, can be blended in for a stunning dining room design.

An Octoberfest table could include a wide, triangular arrangement of gold, orange, and yellow chrysanthemums and an abundance of marigolds with spiky cattails as extenders. Set bunches of artificial green and red grapes at the base of the vase. Surround the display with three tapered candles at the triangular points to complete an elegant, formal arrangement that will carry your table into winter.

WINTER

In most parts of the world, winter signifies a limited supply of available floral components. With artificial flowers, however, your winter arrangements can be as abundant, fresh, and varied as during the spring and summer. Create stunning new de-

Ikebana-inspired, this design featuring Tokyo chrysanthemums is very "new wave." The individual chrysanthemum heads stand like flaming stars in a celestial landscape. Holly branches jut out at sharp angles throughout. The overall effect is startling and unique, a contemporary touch of winter.

signs by mixing year-round flowers with typical winter evergreens, fruit-tree and berry branches, holly, and poinsettias.

Let evergreens supply the green usually provided by foliage in a design of Gerbera daisies. Display pine and spruce boughs enlivened with pine-cones and holly. Bunch some bright red camellia or pink poinsettias at the center of this arrangement for a vibrant mix of textures.

A basket of red carnations, curly silver grass, and green foliage set on the coffee table will make a crackling fire on a cold winter's night seem even more radiant and warm. Use a triangular-shaped arrangement of red, white, and orange chrysanthemums and shiny green holly leaves to crown your dining room or holiday buffet table.

Don't think your home must be devoid of flowers in the winter just because fewer flowers bloom. With artificial flowers, you can use your imagination and your resources to create evocative, heartwarming winter designs that remind one that spring is coming.

SPECIAL HOLIDAY LOOKS

The traditional Christmas colors of red, white, and green are featured in this contemporary country basket brimming with seasonal holiday cheer. Fiery red dahlias, free-flowing holly branches, wild red ranunculus, and a red poinsettia crowning the display are barely contained in the basket. The white forget-me-nots and the beauty of a solitary white poinsettia blossom complement and gently tame the wild red flowers. This stunning basket, overflowing with floral rhythm and color, is spectacular in an entrance hall or on the hearth, sharing its vivaciousness and joy with all.

Holidays are excitedly anticipated miniseasons of romantic and religious significance during which themes of love, peace, joy, and renewal permeate special floral arrangements. Often, holiday designs are traditional and include accessories that are specific to each particular occasion. However, artificial flowers allow you to be able to work with more than just the seasonal flowers, so you can be fresh, innovative, and particularly effective in your holiday designs.

CHRISTMAS

Arrangements announcing the message of this festive holiday should be spread through every room in your home, from countertops and tables to corners filled with floral messages of Christmas cheer. From classic arrangements of poinsettia and holly to unexpected designs of tulips and lilies in vibrant Christmas colors, let the joy and warmth of this season echo through your home.

Arrange three pink-and-white poinsettia blossoms at different levels with three bare branches, a sprig of pine, some holly leaves, and three tiny silver ornaments. This is an Oriental twist on a classic arrangement that can be displayed in the hall or on the mantel. Fill a gold-colored compote with cedar foliage in the shape of a miniature Christmas tree and decorate it with red, medium-sized poinsettias, a few holly leaves, and holly berries. Place this elegant faux tree as a welcome in the entranceway of your home. For a beautiful, new look, decorate your real or artificial Christmas tree with baby's breath, red and white ranunculus, pink, white, and red Christmas roses, and berries. Instead of the traditional star at the top, use a giant, white poinsettia blossom.

Decorate large green wreaths that hang on doors and walls with ribbons, baby's breath, red and white ranunculus, tiny pinecones, nuts, bells, and mistletoe. Smaller wreaths of laurel, ivy, magnolias, forget-me-nots, and some tiny golden ornaments will look spectacular when set throughout the home on any available flat surface.

For a Victorian feel, create an enormous Christmas display of extra-large white and red poinsettia blossoms and holly berry branches in a giant

A magnificent, lifelike artificial Christmas tree is wonderfully decorated with flowers instead of the traditional ornaments. Lovely red ranunculus accent the tips of the branches, and holly and baby's breath add subtle dignity to the entire design. A few velvet ribbons, miniature baskets of apples, and a few jolly Santas and other ornaments are all the other decorations that are needed. Here, the tree's regal beauty is best highlighted with natural accessories.

White and silver are the colors of the New Year, and this arrangement embodies the surge of energy this holiday brings. The camellias, each one in a space of its own, appear as resolutions made, while the buds stretch forth like aspirations for the days to come.

pink vase on a matching pink pedestal. Scatter miniature replicas of this breathtaking centerpiece to carry the seasonal tone through your entire home.

Gold bells, red candles, silver ornaments, and frosted branches are perfect accessories to have on hand at this time of the year. With a little ingenuity and a supply of artificial flowers and greens, you can create some lovely Christmas arrangements in minutes.

NEW YEAR'S DAY

White, silver, and green are the traditional colors of the New Year, symbolizing fresh starts and new beginnings. Remove those Christmas displays and herald in the New Year with some inspiring arrangements.

Camellias and gardenias are popular and useful for their colorful blooms. If you haven't used them in a Christmas design, spread them out over some shiny ivy and holly leaves in a shallow dish for a wonderful centerpiece. A spectacular New Year's Day party arrangement features one enor-

Red and white and roses are the classic components of a true love bouquet, and with artificial flowers the message is eternal. This circular design is simple, but very evocative. All the lovely roses need are a few greens to fill them out. The curling ribbon ensures this bouquet will be recognized as a gift of love.

mous white peony at the center to symbolize the New Year. The round shape is established by four medium-sized, white peonies, four large, pink magnolias, and six medium-sized, red hibiscus. This is filled out with red ranunculus, small, white allium, wild pink hyacinth, and small Christmas roses. Red holly berry branches reach outward for depth.

VALENTINE'S DAY

Valentine's Day is the most romantic of holidays, when love is classically expressed in red, pink, and white floral designs. Arrange rosebuds, forget-me-nots, carnations, and bleeding hearts in cupid vases, silver compotes, and epergnes. Use dramatic curved shapes that reflect love and the intertwining of two hearts.

A Victorian bouquet in a porcelain vase should include freesias, lilies, lavender, anemones, rosebuds, blooming roses, and daisies in an impressive display of affection. For an exotic surprise, arrange Gerbera daisies in twin circles. Bisect them with a flowing Hogarth curve of roses and bleed-

Easter is a time to celebrate new life and nature's beauty. Here, a basket of gorgeous spring flowers seem to be reaching for the skies, stretching as they awake from winter slumber. Primula and daisies have been placed at the base of the arrangement, establishing the foundation. Daffodils and crocus emerge next, mirroring their position in nature. The celebration and movement in this design is joyous and contagious; use it to communicate the special feeling of this holiday.

ing hearts. If you have purchased a Valentine's Day gift, such as a ruby ring, a jeweled watch, diamond earrings, or hard-to-get theater tickets, place the gift in the midst of tiny blue and red marguerite daisies arranged in a Limoges porcelain box for an extra-special "I Love You."

EASTER

Easter is a religious holiday that also signals the coming of spring and summer and a renewal of life in nature. Yellow daffodils, white lilies, purple crocuses, and multicolored tulips are nature's own first blooms after the cold of winter. Gather any or all of these into a ribbon-decked basket to welcome sunshine and warm days.

The traditional Easter lily is always magnificent in a crystal vase set on a white tablecloth, with white linen napkins and white dishes. For a more natural-looking arrangement, replace the Easter lilies with lovely, wild calla lilies that are delicate and hopeful. Violets, crocuses, grape hyacinths, daffodils, forsythia, tulips, and pussy willows blend well together in a large container. Set this design on a table

Most brides keep their wedding bouquets, but they must let them wither and dry. With artificial flowers, the arrangement will always look as fresh and alive as it did on the day of the ceremony. This all-white display of magnolia, carnations, stock, miniature roses, wisteria, and baby's breath is perfect as an altar adornment. It can be transferred to the reception table, then cherished for years to come.

or sideboard, and surround the vase with decorated Easter eggs.

BIRTHDAYS AND ANNIVERSARIES

Birthdays and anniversaries will be more exciting to the celebrant when enhanced by a special bouquet or arrangement featuring his or her favorite flowers. For example, the lily of the valley is universally accepted by floral designers as the flower for the month of May; any arrangement for a birthday or anniversary in May should prominently feature these lilies. An extra, added effect can be obtained when a birthstone gift or anniversary symbol is included in the arrangement. For example, an emerald ring would be a perfect companion to a display of lilies of the valley in May. Lists of monthly flowers, birthstones, and anniversary symbols are readily available at your artificial florist or stationery store.

PATRIOTIC DAYS

The patriotic celebration of many

As summer fades and fall begins, the abundance of nature and its providence is celebrated at harvest time. A simple bowl of peaches is transformed to a special holiday arrangement by the addition of a cluster of brilliant daisies in a cornucopia design.

countries' national holidays can be enhanced with an innovative arrangement of artificial flowers reflecting the colors of the national flag. A distinctly American display for Independence Day festivities will include large red zinnias, imperial blue dahlias, and exploding, star-shaped, white chrysanthemums that capture a feeling of joyous exultation. The French Bastille Day celebration in mid-July could be decorated with an arrangement featuring immense, red, Paris roses, a national symbol of the victory of the French people. Accompany the roses with a subdued amount of tiny, trailing white allium and blue sweet williams that flow gently throughout the arrangement to complete the French tricolor. For local holiday celebrations, individual state flowers or colors can be featured. For example, March 2 is the Texas Independence Day and arrangements here should feature the State of Texas flower—the bluebonnet.

The floral designer can be extremely innovative in creating displays that reflect any holiday—from Christmas to Groundhog's Day. Use your supply of flowers and your imagination to make every day a holiday.

ROMANTIC LOOKS

All flowers generally suggest romance. However, your choice of color scheme, containers, flower blends, and accessories will define the degree of romanticism in your arrangement. Elements chosen with a special person in mind embody romance just by the individual tailoring. From a simple bunch of buttercups lovingly handed by a child to his mother to the elegance of a dozen red roses given by a husband to his wife, flowers convey love and affection. And while natural flowers will fade, the romance of a special artificial design will linger, reminding the recipient of a special sentiment between lovers or friends.

Simple arrangements placed in the bedroom, at the dinner table, or near the fireplace can be arranged quickly to add romance to a special evening or occasion. Place six interestingly curved, heavily laden, pink apple blossom branches in a pink vase to invoke a very romantic mood.

Roses are the flowers noted for romantic statements. Pink and red blooms and buds are classically displayed with dark green leaves in a silver or pewter container. For something different, combine three or four large, fully opened, light pink Paris

Nothing is more romantic than to lounge before a fire with a loved one. However, the atmosphere can be enhanced with the addition of an abundance of flowers. Red and white are the colors of love, so this hearth was adorned with an arrangement and a wreath of red and white poinsettias and holly, and a basket of apples and evergreens. Two complementary pillows invite any couple to curl up and enjoy the cozy scene.

121

This classic arrangement of peonies, roses, and crystal glistens with romantic elegance. Gentle baby's breath sparkles throughout the design. Perfect for a dresser, it will warm any heart with its sophisticated simplicity.

roses with a small bunch of dark pink rosebuds. Bend the stems so they are very short and arrange all the roses and buds closely together in a shallow container. You can also lovingly group roses of vastly contrasting colors and sizes together in a romantic display a designer has labeled "Fireworks."

One kind of flower in all its colors is another extremely effective romantic look. Place a number of Michaelmas daisies in many shades of deep pink together in a balloon vase. Arrange the deep pink shades in the center of the arrangement and the light pink shades toward the outside to suggest a radiating burst of color. Sprinkle tiny, white ranunculus throughout. This dramatic look is especially romantic when massed to cover an entire table, with blooms hanging over the table's edge and others spiraling upward in an explosion of pink.

Many designs employ a romantic container with complementary flowers to suggest a period or mood. For example, a rectangular, porcelain container painted with green foliage and pink, blue, and gold flowers is romantic in itself; the bouquet placed

Hydrangea is the classic flower of the Victorian age, a rich and sentimental time. Enclosed here in a replica of a period basket, hydrangea evoke the romance of this era. The way the blossoms are bunched reminds one of the overstuffed parlors, and the contrast of the blooms to the slick leaves reflects the mix of textures characteristic of Victorian interior design.

in it need only reflect the painted design. Spade-shaped, glossy green ivy at the base of the arrangement, with lavender irises, blue violets, pink hyacinth, and pink and white scabiosa topped with yellow and white daisies and white orchids will produce a vertical mirror reflection of the vase. Placed on a glass coffee table in front of a white sectional sofa set, the romantic warmth of this vase and its floral reflection will become the breathtaking decorative center of attention in the room.

Flowers carefully chosen for one special person or situation automatically become romantic and evocative. A loving husband serves his wife breakfast in bed on a pink-and-green flowered tray with matching linen napkins. Beside the bed he sets an arrangement of tiny white violets, large, dramatic, Tokyo roses, miniature, pale purple and yellow orchids, pink scabiosa, and pink lilies. They are gathered in a wicker basket painted pink and green to match the linen and the tray. No more need be said or done to articulate special feelings of love, caring, and affection.

This lovely arrangement has been carefully designed as the finishing touch to the romantic theme of this room. The mix of chintzes is joined by a circular display of roses, primroses, sweetpeas, and anemones. The mass arrangement carefully reflects the flowers in the fabric patterns.

Although classic romantic arrangements employ shades of pink, red, and white, personalization and creativity will often be more effective for a long-remembered, meaningful statement. A wife designs an arrangement of field flowers for her husband's den that reflects his love of hunting and fishing. Giant yellow ranunculus, beige field thistles, brown cattails, red and purple clover, white arrowheads, and bleached palm spears are gathered in a natural wicker tackle box with an open lid. On the table, emerging from under the palm spears that hang over the edge of the tackle box, are two hand-carved hunting dogs, one pointing and the other flushing birds.

Accessories reflecting the tastes of the recipient or gifts to be shared with the giver will romanticize an arrangement, too. A bottle of champagne, a delicious box of chocolate truffles, or some fragrant perfumes and bath soaps nestled in a basket of pink violets and roses, and tied with large trailing pink and white ribbons will leave no chance for an expression of love to be misunderstood.

Spring is a time of romance and renewed love, so here is an arrangement that celebrates the flowers of spring. Peonies, dahlias, and lilies massed in the middle of this triangular form, take center stage in tints of pink and white. They are complemented and enhanced by blossoming almond, budding snapdragons, and awakening orchids. Unopened buds reach everywhere, promising beauty and romance all summer long.

A CATALOGUE OF ARTIFICIAL FLOWERS

There is a surprisingly vast variety of artificial flowers produced in the world today. Modeled on actual wildflowers and cultivated flowers in a rainbow assortment of colors, tints, and hues, this exciting diversity and adaptability has created a "new nature." A visit to an artificial flower market is an exciting look into this new world, where the floral imagination is not limited by the availability or seasonality of a certain flower. Here, one can choose blossoms in refreshingly new combinations that make dramatic design statements.

This accompanying catalogue displays only a sample of the artificial flowers available. Most are exact duplications of their natural counterparts, although a few are interesting combinations of similar species. Look closely at the catalogue, for the reality of these artificial flowers is breathtaking. Use the catalogue, too, to carefully plan your floral designs and purchases.

AFRICAN DAISY

BOTANICAL NAME:
Arctotis breviscapa; Compositae

COMMON NAME:
African daisy

SEASON:
Late spring and summer

COLORS:
Yellow, deep red

SPECIAL INSTRUCTIONS:
The African daisy fits well in all design styles as a focal or supporting flower. It mixes especially beautifully with red anemones.

SENTIMENT:
Innocence

AGAPANTHUS

BOTANICAL NAME:
Agapanthus africanus; Liliaceae

COMMON NAME:
Agapanthus; African lily

SEASON:
Spring and summer

COLORS:
Blue, white, yellow, dark lilac

SPECIAL INSTRUCTIONS:
Agapanthus is a dramatic flower that works best in Japanese, large mass, and contemporary designs. Arrange blue agapanthus in a porcelain container of matching colors with deep purple and mauve gladiolus, burgundy onion heads, and pale mauve carnations for a stunning display of blues.

SENTIMENT:
Sweetness

ALMOND

BOTANICAL NAME:
Prunus amygdalus; Rosaceae

COMMON NAME:
Almond; flowering almond

SEASON:
Spring

COLORS:
White, pink

SPECIAL INSTRUCTIONS:
Almonds can be an unexpected addition to an arrangement. They are especially intriguing when scented with almond essence.

SENTIMENT:
Hope

ALSTROEMERIA

BOTANICAL NAME:
Alstroemeria pelegrina; Liliaceae

COMMON NAME:
Alstroemeria; Peruvian lily

SEASON:
All year

COLORS:
Yellow, rust, orange, gold, red, pink

SPECIAL INSTRUCTIONS:
Alstroemeria look like miniature lilies. Use them to fill in the spaces in a mass arrangement.

SENTIMENT:
Revitalization

BABY'S BREATH

BOTANICAL NAME:
Gypsophila paniculata; Caryophyllaceae

COMMON NAME:
Baby's breath

SEASON:
All year

COLORS:
White, pink, blue

SPECIAL INSTRUCTIONS:
Baby's breath is one of the most commonly used fillers because its twinkling, soft clustery effect blends well with all designs and flowers.

SENTIMENT:
Lasting beauty

BACCHARIS

BOTANICAL NAME:
Baccharis halimifolia; Compositae

COMMON NAME:
Baccharis; Lady's glove; Clown's spikenard

SEASON:
Autumn

COLORS:
White, silver, gray

SPECIAL INSTRUCTIONS:
Fluffy baccharis is a terrific filler flower. The silver blooms will enhance a New Year arrangement.

SENTIMENT:
Modesty

BOUGAINVILLEA

BOTANICAL NAME:
Bougainvillea buttiana; Nyctaginaceae

COMMON NAME:
Bougainvillea

SEASON:
Summer

COLORS:
Lilac, pink, white, red, orange

SPECIAL INSTRUCTIONS:
Bougainvillea are especially good for
arrangements of the Hogarth curve or to add
proportion to other arrangements. They can
also be featured dramatically alone as a hanging
plant.

SENTIMENT:
Romance

BUTTERCUP

BOTANICAL NAME:
Ranunculus acris; Ranunculaceae

COMMON NAME:
Buttercup; Ranunculus

SEASON:
All year

COLORS:
Yellow, white, red, burgundy

SPECIAL INSTRUCTIONS:
The buttercup's natural wildness is wonderful
in country arrangements in baskets, but it also
can be used in contemporary design as a filler.
Another alternative is to show yellow buttercups
alone in a blue container.

SENTIMENT:
Ingratitude

CAMPANULA

BOTANICAL NAME:
Campanula grandiflora; Campanulaceae

COMMON NAME:
Campanula; Bellflower; Bluebell

SEASON:
Spring and summer

COLORS:
Violet, purple, pink, white

SPECIAL INSTRUCTIONS:
Campanula is an alpine flower that is fitting for period and traditional arrangements. The purple variety is stunning with tawny orange alstroemeria.

SENTIMENT:
Gratitude

CENTAURY

BOTANICAL NAME:
Centaurium erythraea; Gentianaceae

COMMON NAME:
Centaury

SEASON:
June through September

COLORS:
Bright red, pale blue, deep blue, yellow-orange

SPECIAL INSTRUCTIONS:
Centaury is a wildflower for European country designs that also works well as a filler in contemporary arrangements. It mixes with orange marigolds and blue larkspur.

SENTIMENT:
Hope in love

CHRISTMAS ROSE

BOTANICAL NAME:
Helleborus niger; Ranunculaceae

COMMON NAME:
Christmas rose

SEASON:
Winter

COLORS:
White (pure and tinged with pink)

SPECIAL INSTRUCTIONS:
The Christmas rose is a magnificent focal flower for traditional and contemporary Christmas and winter arrangements. It also works well in Japanese designs.

SENTIMENT:
Peace amidst confusion

CLIMBING ROSE

BOTANICAL NAME:
Rosa sempervirens; Rosaceae

COMMON NAME:
Climbing rose

SEASON:
June to October

COLORS:
Pink, red, white, yellow, orange

SPECIAL INSTRUCTIONS:
Climbing roses are immense blooms that work with almost all flowers and designs, therefore, they are used more often than any other kind of rose.

SENTIMENT:
Love

COSMOS

BOTANICAL NAME:
Cosmos bipinnatus; Compositae

COMMON NAME:
Cosmos

SEASON:
Summer and autumn

COLORS:
White, rose, orange, red, yellow

SPECIAL INSTRUCTIONS:
Cosmos are lovely with marigolds, zinnias, and
tall, spiky flowers in a garden arrangement.

SENTIMENT:
Missing loved ones or friends

CROCUS

BOTANICAL NAME:
Crocus chrysanthus; Iridaceae

COMMON NAME:
Crocus; Saffron crocus

SEASON:
Winter; early spring

COLORS:
Blue, purple, white, yellow, red, pink

SPECIAL INSTRUCTIONS:
Crocus can wake up a tired winter arrangement
with their bright pastel colors.

SENTIMENT:
Impatience

CYMBIDIUM ORCHID

BOTANICAL NAME:
Cymbidium Babylon orchis; Orchidaceae

COMMON NAME:
Cymbidium orchid

SEASON:
All year

COLORS:
Many colors

SPECIAL INSTRUCTIONS:
The cymbidium orchid is a superb focal flower that mixes well with other kinds of orchids and with roses.

SENTIMENT:
Beauty

DAFFODIL

BOTANICAL NAME:
Narcissus pseudonarcissus; Amaryllidaceae

COMMON NAME:
Daffodil; Narcissus; Jonquil

SEASON:
Early spring

COLORS:
White, yellow, variegated

SPECIAL INSTRUCTIONS:
Daffodils are tremendous with other spring flowers, such as violets, irises, tulips, and snapdragons. However, they will lighten any dark color scheme, adding sunshine and radiance. They look especially lovely with wild arum, cowslips, and grape hyacinths.

SENTIMENT:
False hope

DAHLIA

BOTANICAL NAME:
Dahlia variabilis; Compositae

COMMON NAME:
Dahlia

SEASON:
Spring to autumn

COLORS:
Many colors

SPECIAL INSTRUCTIONS:
Dahlias can be nobly displayed in traditional mass, line, and contemporary arrangements in all color schemes.

SENTIMENT:
Instability

FLOWERING RUSH

BOTANICAL NAME:
Butomus umbellatus; Butomaceae

COMMON NAME:
Flowering rush; Water gladiolus

SEASON:
Spring, summer, and autumn

COLORS:
Yellow, pink, purple, red, white, variegated

SPECIAL INSTRUCTIONS:
Often used magnificently as a filler in European designs, this delicate cluster can also be featured in contemporary design.

SENTIMENT:
Achievement

FORGET-ME-NOT

BOTANICAL NAME:
Myosotis alpestris; Boraginaceae

COMMON NAME:
Forget-me-not

SEASON:
Spring and summer

COLORS:
White, azure, rose pink

SPECIAL INSTRUCTIONS:
Forget-me-nots are often used as filler, but they
mix well in all arrangements. For instance, they
take on a classic flair in a Victorian
arrangement with lilacs, carnations, Queen
Anne's lace, blue hydrangea, and thistle in a
white china vase.

SENTIMENT:
True love

FREESIA

BOTANICAL NAME:
Freesia hybrida; Iridaceae

COMMON NAME:
Freesia

SEASON:
All year

COLORS:
White, red, purple, yellow, orange

SPECIAL INSTRUCTIONS:
Freesia are perfect in miniature arrangements.
They also look great with daffodils and
hyacinths in a clear glass container.

SENTIMENT:
Love at first sight

FUCHSIA

BOTANICAL NAME:
Fuchsia hybrida; Onagraceae

COMMON NAME:
Fuchsia

SEASON:
Summer

COLORS:
Red, white, lilac, pink

SPECIAL INSTRUCTIONS:
Fuchsia is an arresting hanging flower that mixes well with roses, peonies, privet, rosemary, and chrysanthemums in a spectacular color display.

SENTIMENT:
Love is blind

GERANIUM

BOTANICAL NAME:
Pelargonium domesticum; Geraniaceae

COMMON NAME:
Geranium

SEASON:
Spring to autumn

COLORS:
Red, white, yellow, pink, purple

SPECIAL INSTRUCTIONS:
Geraniums are generally used in traditional, contemporary, and period—especially early American designs. They also mix well with irises and agapanthus in terra-cotta and ceramic containers.

SENTIMENT:
Expected meeting

GLOXINIA

BOTANICAL NAME:
Sinningia speciosa; Gesneriaceae

COMMON NAME:
Gloxinia

SEASON:
Summer and autumn

COLORS:
Red, violet, lavender, white, yellow

SPECIAL INSTRUCTIONS:
Gloxinia is a flowering houseplant rich in texture and interest. This replica is so perfect it should be featured alone.

SENTIMENT:
Favor

HIBISCUS

BOTANICAL NAME:
Hibiscus syriacus; Malvaceae

COMMON NAME:
Hibiscus; Rose of Sharon

SEASON:
Summer to autumn

COLORS:
Many colors

SPECIAL INSTRUCTIONS:
Hibiscus is often used in mass arrangements, and mixes particularly well with irises, larkspur, chrysanthemums, pompoms, and stock.

SENTIMENT:
Symbol of resurrection

HYACINTH

BOTANICAL NAME:
Hyacinthus orientalis; Liliaceae

COMMON NAME:
Hyacinth

SEASON:
Early spring

COLORS:
White, pink, deep purple-blue, dark blue

SPECIAL INSTRUCTIONS:
Hyacinth is a popular Victorian flower that is outstanding in arrangements for period and traditional settings. For an outdoor display, mix it with yellow freesias, red and purple anemones, violets, and roses in a white vase.

SENTIMENT:
Sorrow

HYDRANGEA

BOTANICAL NAME:
Hydrangea macrophylla; Saxifragaceae

COMMON NAME:
Hydrangea

SEASON:
Summer and autumn

COLORS:
Many colors

SPECIAL INSTRUCTIONS:
Use hydrangea flowers and leaves in contemporary arrangements; the leaves will add a glossy textured backdrop for the flowers' grandeur. Place multicolored hydrangea in an oblong bowl with a few leaves interspersed, or arrange a few blossoms in various colors with pink phlox, blue thistle, and deep purple salvia.

SENTIMENT:
Boasting

IRIS

BOTANICAL NAME:
Iris xiphium; Iridaceae

COMMON NAME:
Iris; Spanish iris

SEASON:
Spring

COLORS:
Purple, yellow, white

SPECIAL INSTRUCTIONS:
Irises are dramatic flowers for all styles and designs and add color and height. They look great with larkspur, lilies, daffodils.

SENTIMENT:
A special message

LARKSPUR

BOTANICAL NAME:
Delphinium grandiflorum; Ranunculaceae

COMMON NAME:
Larkspur; Delphinium

SEASON:
May to August

COLORS:
White, dark blue, lavender

SPECIAL INSTRUCTIONS:
Larkspur mix well with lilies, daisies, snapdragons, irises, and stock in country-garden arrangements.

SENTIMENT:
Levity

LIATRIS

BOTANICAL NAME:
Liatris spicata; Compositae

COMMON NAME:
Liatrus; Blazing star

SEASON:
June through December

COLORS:
Lavender

SPECIAL INSTRUCTIONS:
Liatris are good extender flowers in mass arrangements.

SENTIMENT:
Magic

LILAC

BOTANICAL NAME:
Syringa vulgaris; Oleaceae

COMMON NAME:
Lilac

SEASON:
November to May

COLORS:
White, blue, purple, lavender, pink

SPECIAL INSTRUCTIONS:
Lilac is a wonderful, spiky flower that fits naturally into classic, country, and contemporary styles, and mixes especially well with roses.

SENTIMENT:
Young love

LINUM

BOTANICAL NAME:
Linum anglicum; Linaceae

COMMON NAME:
Linum; Linaigrette; Flax

SEASON:
Summer to autumn

COLORS:
Blue, pale blue, bright red, yellow-orange

SPECIAL INSTRUCTIONS:
Linum is a wildflower perfect for miniature arrangements. It is also great as an unusual filler.

SENTIMENT:
Smoothness

LOTUS

BOTANICAL NAME:
Nymphaea odorata; Nymphaeaceae

COMMON NAME:
Lotus; Water lily

SEASON:
Summer

COLORS:
White, red, yellow, pink

SPECIAL INSTRUCTIONS:
Lotus are displayed most effectively alone with foliage, on a mirror, or in a simple Oriental design.

SENTIMENT:
Lost love

MADONNA LILY

BOTANICAL NAME:
Lilium candidum; Liliaceae

COMMON NAME:
Madonna lily

SEASON:
Summer

COLORS:
White

SPECIAL INSTRUCTIONS:
Use Madonna lilies with irises and freesia in a classic triangle.

SENTIMENT:
Purity

MAGNOLIA

BOTANICAL NAME:
Magnolia soulangeana; Magnoliaceae

COMMON NAME:
Magnolia; Saucer magnolia

SEASON:
Early spring

COLORS:
White, pink, yellow, purple, rose

SPECIAL INSTRUCTIONS:
Magnolia are extremely popular in Oriental designs, but are also terrific when mixed with peonies, tulips, irises, and campanula.

SENTIMENT:
Magnificence

MARIGOLD

BOTANICAL NAME:
Calendula officinalis; Compositae

COMMON NAME:
Marigold

SEASON:
June to September

COLORS:
Many colors

SPECIAL INSTRUCTIONS:
Marigolds are bold, contemporary flowers used most effectively to brighten an arrangement.

SENTIMENT:
Contempt

MICHAELMAS DAISY

BOTANICAL NAME:
Aster novae-belgii; Compositae

COMMON NAME:
Michaelmas daisy; Aster

SEASON:
Summer and autumn

COLORS:
Orange, white, pink, lavender, purple, red

SPECIAL INSTRUCTIONS:
The Michaelmas daisy is a strong form flower in colors that mix well with marigolds, zinnias, snapdragons, and irises.

SENTIMENT:
Simplicity

MIMOSA

BOTANICAL NAME:
Acacia dealbata; Mimosaceae

COMMON NAME:
Mimosa

SEASON:
Late winter and spring

COLORS:
Yellow

SPECIAL INSTRUCTIONS:
The sprays of the globular mimosa flowers are exotic for Oriental lines and gorgeous with evergreen fillers in winter arrangements.

SENTIMENT:
Women's emancipation

NASTURTIUM

BOTANICAL NAME:
Tropaeolum majus; Tropaeolaceae

COMMON NAME:
Nasturtium

SEASON:
Summer and autumn

COLORS:
Bright yellow, deep orange, white

SPECIAL INSTRUCTIONS:
Nasturtiums are magnificent supporting flowers in period designs.

SENTIMENT:
Patriotism

PARIS ROSE

BOTANICAL NAME:
Rosa polyantha; Rosaceae

COMMON NAME:
Paris rose; Queen Elizabeth rose

SEASON:
Spring to autumn

COLORS:
Pink, red, white

SPECIAL INSTRUCTIONS:
The miniature Paris roses are superb in classic
French and Victorian design. They also work
well with irises, larkspur, pompoms, and other
kinds of roses.

SENTIMENT:
Love

PEONY

BOTANICAL NAME:
Paeonia lactiflora; Paeoniaceae

COMMON NAME:
Peony

SEASON:
May to June

COLORS:
Many colors

SPECIAL INSTRUCTIONS:
The peony is a large form flower whose size and
color can be the focal point for a garden
arrangement of lilies and white lilacs, or as an
accompaniment to zinnias, campanula, daucus,
and blue irises.

SENTIMENT:
Happiness

POINSETTIA

BOTANICAL NAME:
Euphorbia pulcherrima; Euphorbiaceae

COMMON NAME:
Poinsettia

SEASON:
Winter

COLORS:
Red, white, pink

SPECIAL INSTRUCTIONS:
Poinsettia is the most popular Christmas flower. It can be displayed alone or mixed with evergreens for a fresh Christmas look.

SENTIMENT:
Hope

PRIMROSE

BOTANICAL NAME:
Primula polyantha; Primulaceae

COMMON NAME:
Primrose

SEASON:
Spring

COLORS:
Red, yellow, white, pink, purple, orange

SPECIAL INSTRUCTIONS:
Primroses are miniatures that look great when grouped in one color alone, but can also be mixed in a variety of colors in a small pot. You can also plant them at the foot of an artificial tree to appear as if they are growing out of the moss.

SENTIMENT:
Sadness

QUEEN ANNE'S LACE

BOTANICAL NAME:
Daucus carota; Umbelliferae

COMMON NAME:
Queen Anne's lace; Wild carrot; Daucus

SEASON:
Late summer

COLORS:
White, cream

SPECIAL INSTRUCTIONS:
Queen Anne's lace is an arranger's staple, marvelous in all designs, especially Victorian and country, as a great filler.

SENTIMENT:
Patience

RANUNCULUS

BOTANICAL NAME:
Ranunculus lingua; Ranunculaceae

COMMON NAME:
Ranunculus; Buttercups

SEASON:
Spring

COLORS:
Red, yellow, orange

SPECIAL INSTRUCTIONS:
Ranunculus is a wonderful artificial flower. The natural blossom is very poisonous and cannot be used as often as this beautiful flower should be.

SENTIMENT:
Stillness

RASPBERRY

BOTANICAL NAME:
Rubus deliciosus; Rosaceae

COMMON NAME:
Raspberry; Bramble

SEASON:
Spring to autumn

COLORS:
White blooms with red berries

SPECIAL INSTRUCTIONS:
Raspberries are particularly effective as a
texture element. The berries provide a shining
burst of color.

SENTIMENT:
A delicacy

RHODODENDRON

BOTANICAL NAME:
Azalea mollis; Ericaceae

COMMON NAME:
Rhododendron

SEASON:
Spring

COLORS:
Red, yellow, white, pink, orange

SPECIAL INSTRUCTIONS:
Originally Oriental, the rhododendron clusters
are perfect alone or as focal flowers for ikebana
arrangements.

SENTIMENT:
Danger

SNAPDRAGON

BOTANICAL NAME:
Antirrhinum majus; Scrophulariaceae

COMMON NAME:
Snapdragon

SEASON:
Spring to autumn

COLORS:
Red, yellow, orange, pink, white

SPECIAL INSTRUCTIONS:
Snapdragon is the perfect line flower that mixes well in large arrangements featuring large focal flowers.

SENTIMENT:
Presumption

SUMMER LILY

BOTANICAL NAME:
Lilium speciosum; Liliaceae

COMMON NAME:
Summer lily

SEASON:
Summer

COLORS:
White, pink

SPECIAL INSTRUCTIONS:
Summer lilies are great in period and contemporary arrangements. They look superb with roses, freesia, and Queen Anne's lace.

SENTIMENT:
Majesty

SWEET PEA

BOTANICAL NAME:
Lathyrus odoratus; Papilionaceae

COMMON NAME:
Sweet pea

SEASON:
Spring

COLORS:
Many colors

SPECIAL INSTRUCTIONS:
Sweet pea are wonderful alone or in a spring bouquet with roses and violets.

SENTIMENT:
Departure

THISTLE

BOTANICAL NAME:
Cirsium lanceolatum; Compositae

COMMON NAME:
Thistle

SEASON:
July to September

COLORS:
Light magenta, lilac, white

SPECIAL INSTRUCTIONS:
The thistle is a country wildflower. It is most often used for color and its superbly rich texture. Set off the color and texture with daisies, sanguisorbas, pink lilies, and white pompoms.

SENTIMENT:
Austerity

TOKYO CHRYSANTHEMUM

BOTANICAL NAME:
Chrysanthemum indicum; Compositae

COMMON NAME:
Tokyo chrysanthemum

SEASON:
Autumn and winter

COLORS:
Yellow, white, pink, burnt orange

SPECIAL INSTRUCTIONS:
The Tokyo chrysanthemum is a large focal flower perfect for Oriental designs. It can also be used with snapdragons in contemporary displays.

SENTIMENT:
Cheerfulness

TULIP

BOTANICAL NAME:
Tulipa gesneriana; Liliaceae

COMMON NAME:
Tulip

SEASON:
Spring

COLORS:
Many colors

SPECIAL INSTRUCTIONS:
The tulip is a spectacular, glossy, spring flower used with lilies, daffodils, hyacinth, and irises.

SENTIMENT:
New love

WHEAT

BOTANICAL NAME:
Triticum aestivum; Gramineae

COMMON NAME:
Wheat

SEASON:
All year

COLORS:
Green, brown, mauve, lavender, gold

SPECIAL INSTRUCTIONS:
Wheat is a common filler for field arrangements
or for a touch of country in a classical
arrangement.

SENTIMENT:
Riches

WILD ASTER

BOTANICAL NAME:
Aster thomsonii; Compositae

COMMON NAME:
Wild aster

SEASON:
All year

COLORS:
All colors

SPECIAL INSTRUCTIONS:
The wild aster is a field flower that is wonderful
as the focal point of wildflower arrangements.

SENTIMENT:
Diversity

WISTERIA

BOTANICAL NAME:
Wisteria sinensis; Papilionaceae

COMMON NAME:
Wisteria

SEASON:
Spring

COLORS:
White, mauve

SPECIAL INSTRUCTIONS:
The wisteria is a beautiful climbing vine for columns and trellises. The branches may also be used in large arrangements that need a hanging thrust below the top of the pot.

SENTIMENT:
Welcome

SOURCES AND USEFUL ADDRESSES

All the Un Jardin...en Plus artificial flowers
shown in this book are available by mail order from:

Huguette Doulmet
19 rue de Chartres
92400 Courbevoie
Paris France
47 89 08 42

Many artificial flower arrangers find it convenient
to buy in quantity and then divide the supply
among themselves.
In addition, Un Jardin...en Plus concept stores
are featured in department stores and boutiques
all around the U.S., Canada, and the U.K. For
information regarding a concept store in your
area, please call the number above, or:

Un Jardin...en Plus
24 West 57th Street
New York, New York 10019
(212) 489-9760

UNITED STATES SOURCES AND USEFUL ADDRESSES

Other artificial flower products and supplies are
available from:

Containers

Milton Adler
501 Madison Avenue
Atlantic City, NJ 08401

Balos
2720 North Paulina Street
Chicago, IL 60614

The Blenko Glass Co.
P.O. Box 67
Milton, WV 22541

E.O. Brody
P.O. Box 22180
Cleveland, OH 44122

Davidson-Uphoff, Inc.
P.O. Box 184
Clarendon Hills, IL 60514

Franklin China
112 Terwood Road
Willow Grove, PA 19090

Hoosier Glass
P.O. Box 756
Kokomo, IN 46901

Vincent Lippe
11 East 26th Street
New York, NY 10010

Mottahedeh
225 Fifth Avenue
New York, NY 10010

Riekes-Crisa Corp.
1818 Leavenworth Street
Omaha, NB 68102

Toscany Imports, Ltd.
245 Fifth Avenue
New York, NY 10016

Toyo Trading Co.
13000 Spring Street
Los Angeles, CA 90061

Dried Materials

Knud Nielsen Co.
P.O. Box 746
Evergreen, AL 36401

Vans, Inc.
3730 West 131st Street
Alsip, IL 60658

Accessories and Other Supplies

Kurt Adler, Inc.—Christmas supplies
1107 Broadway
New York, NY 10010

Best Buy Floral Supply
P.O. Box 1982
Cedar Rapids, IO 52406

Design Master Floral Products
P.O. Box 601
Boulder, CO 80306

Fibre-Form Products
329 Town & Country Village
Palo Alto, CA 94301

Floral Masters International
1111 Hawthorne Lane, Bldg. D
P.O. Box 100
Wheeling, IL 60090

Florists Products
2242 North Palmer Drive
Schaumberg, IL 60195

J.M. Trading Corp.
241 Frontage Road, Suite 31
Burr Ridge, IL 60521

Lomey Florist Supplies
301 Suburban Avenue
P.O. Box 7
Deer Park, NY 11729

Schattur Novelty Corp.
901 Broadway
New York, NY 10003

Schusters of Texas, Inc.
Box 97
Goldthwaite, TX 76844

Union County Florist Supplies, Inc.
87 Grove Avenue
Staten Island, NY 10302

UNITED KINGDOM SOURCES AND USEFUL ADDRESSES

Un Jardin...en Plus products can be ordered through:

Nina Campbell Ltd.
9 Walton Street
London SW3
Tel: 01 225 1011

Other artificial flower products and supplies are available from:

Clifton Nurseries
5A Clifton Villas
Warwick Avenue
London W9

Clifton Nurseries
16 Russell Street
Covent Garden
London WC2

D.H. Evans
318 Oxford Street
London W1

Floral Design
London House
26-40 Kensington High Street
London W8

John Groom's Craft Centre
Edgware Way
Edgware
Middlesex

Harrods
Knightsbridge
London SW1

Jeannette Norell Ltd.
79 Elizabeth Street
London SW1

Peter Jones
Sloane Square
London SW1

John Lewis
Oxford Street
London W1

Neal Street East
5 Neal Street
Covent Garden
London WC2

Oasis Art Flora
194/196 Walton Street
London SW3

Plantation
200 Battersea Park Road
London SW11

Selfridges Ltd.
Oxford Street
London W1

AUSTRALIAN SOURCES AND USEFUL ADDRESSES

Un Jardin...en Plus artificial flowers are stocked by:

Sacaro
23/25 Bay Street
Double Bay
Sydney
2028 NSW
Tel: Sydney 328 68 19

INDEX